For dear Judy
with love from Gyles.
Christmas 1992.

A MATTER OF DEATH AND LIFE
A record of true experiences

A MATTER OF DEATH AND LIFE

A record of true experiences

Gyles Adams

Foreword by
Canon Ian Collins

The Book Guild Ltd
Sussex, England

This book is sold subject to the condition that it shall not, by way of trade or otherwise, be lent, re-sold, hired out, photocopied or held in any retrieval system, or otherwise circulated without the publisher's prior consent in any form of binding or cover other than that in which this is published and without a similar condition including this condition being imposed on the subsequent purchaser.

The Book Guild Limited
25 High Street
Lewes, Sussex
First Published 1991
© Gyles Adams 1991
Set in Baskerville
Typesetting by Cable Graphics
Eastbourne, East Sussex
Printed in Great Britain by
Antony Rowe Ltd,
Chippenham, Wiltshire

British Library Cataloguing in Publication Data
Adams, Gyles 1910-
    A matter of death and life: a record of true experiences.
    1. Spiritualism. Mediums. Biographies.
    I. Title
    133.91092
ISBN 0 86332 592 0

*All Seekers after the Truth
are welcome here.*

CONTENTS

Foreword	9
Introduction	11
A Matter of Death And Life	17
Chapter One	33
Chapter Two	41
Chapter Three	49
Chapter Four	59
Chapter Five	68
Chapter Six	75
Chapter Seven	82
Chapter Eight	92
Chapter Nine	102
Chapter Ten	111
Chapter Eleven	120
Chapter Twelve	131
Postscript	139

FOREWORD

by
Canon Collins
Formerly of St George's Chapel, Windsor Castle

There are signs that there is an awakening of interest in things spiritual. This is linked with a recognition by more and more people that materialism and scientific progress cannot bring about man's salvation. This is not to say that people are flocking back to orthodox religion, rather, they are seeking deeper values and truths outside the organised churches. There is a feeling that there are a great many different ways of experiencing things spiritual. As St Paul says:

> 'There are varieties of gifts, but the same spirit;
> there are varieties of service, but the same Lord.'
> (I Corinthians 12.4-5)

The pages that follow are an account of one man's encounters with things of the Spirit. They tell how the author came to recognise the value and force of things spiritual, which changed his whole life and outlook and completely altered his attitude and approach to his fellow men. This is a very personal account of extraordinary revelations, born of a tragic friendship, which led him to an intense realisation of the life to come and its importance in relation to the present.

I have known Gyles Adams for many years and can vouch for his sincerity. I have seen the fruits of his gifts — his concern and love for his fellows, especially those less fortunate, and witnessed his dedication to their help by his prayers and actions. All this as a result of strange and wonderful experiences which he now shares with others that they, too, may come to an awareness of the spiritual qualities of life, and be helped by them.

Ian G. Collins.
Southwell,
Nottinghamshire.

INTRODUCTION

Returning from America in 1950, I stayed for a short while with my sister and her husband at Lea Farm Cottage, in a remote part of Berkshire. It was not a cottage in the true sense, but part of a large Victorian farmhouse — and the most memorable thing about it was the fact that it was haunted.

My sister knew a little of its history. The farm had been owned by two sisters, but after a bitter quarrel they decided not to live together, and divided the house between them. One had lived at the front, with her own piece of land, and the other at the back, again with her own garden. In this way they were totally independent and need never meet.

Years passed, but the fact that they were growing old did not persuade them to end their isolation. Then, without warning, one died. It was, apparently, a heart attack while picking gooseberries from a bush some hundred yards from the door. Who found her, and how long she remained undiscovered, is anyone's guess, but it was she who haunted the part of the house in which I stayed.

It would have been interesting to know more of the sad story. What had been the cause of the quarrel which led to such a long, lonely silence? How had the remaining sister felt on hearing of the tragedy? The only thing we knew was that she had sold the entire property and moved away — but the house remained divided because the new owner did not need as many rooms.

We were never told the names of those unhappy women, and were not sufficiently curious to inquire. My sister referred to her ghost as 'Old Ada', simply because it was a country name which appeared suitable for the small, dumpy woman who still visited the double bedroom.

'Small and dumpy' was the best description my sister could come up with. She never really saw her face (possibly because she was reluctant to take a close look). Ada would announce her presence with a curious 'vibration', a 'throbbing in the atmosphere' which could be felt and almost heard. Then wisps of mist would gather in a corner of the room and the old lady appear, moving in the midst of them. Sometimes the fog would so arrange itself that only the head and feet were visible, and at other times it would be another section of her body. Always the short, squat figure was shrouded in shadowy mist.

My sister was not frightened, but after a while she did admit that Ada was getting on her nerves, and she would not go up to bed unless her husband went with her. Since we were not particularly religious, it did not occur to us to pray for this restless spirit, or seek a minister to perform an exorcism, but my brother-in-law knew a young couple who suggested they might help, and it was arranged that they should visit us.

I cannot recall the names of the young people, neither do I remember anything of their appearance, but the outcome of their visit remains vividly in my memory. To put it briefly: they 'did the glass'. This is a crude, sometimes effective and often dangerous method of contacting 'the other side'. It was the first time I'd encountered the procedure.

A small round table in a downstair room was considered suitable for the purpose. After the surface had been polished, letters were arranged around the circumference in alphabetical order, and an upturned tumbler placed in the centre. Then the five of us sat around, each placing a finger on the base of the glass. Then we waited, and waited, arms aching until we were obliged to change hands, again and again.

We were about to abandon the experiment when the glass suddenly 'took off'. It shot to the letter A and then moved rapidly from one letter to the next until the alphabet was completed. It was all we could do to keep our fingers on the glass.

'Would you tell us your name?' asked one of the visitors, in a voice that trembled a little.

The glass responded with alacrity, going to E, then L and I.

'Eliza' guessed my brother-in-law, but it hadn't finished. It was to spell the full name 'Elizabeth'. Then, after a brief pause, it began again M - A - R —

'Mary' guessed someone, but it was 'Martha'. Then, most surprising of all, it added a long and unusual surname.

'I'm sure it's Ada,' said my sister, and immediately the glass moved again. 'Yes — Ada'.

It was tremendously exciting. Too exciting for our visitors. To my surprise and disappointment, they removed their fingers from the glass and declared that they thought it unwise to continue. I think they were frightened, for while they had used the glass before they had never met with such a strong response. Since they were our guests, we could not help but accept their decision.

But if I had known then what I was to learn later, I could not, and would not, have let the matter rest in such an unsatisfactory manner. We should have sought the answers to the questions. Why was Ada haunting the farmhouse? Why had she wanted to make contact with us? My guess would be that she could not find rest before making peace with her sister — and that lady was still alive and living in the district.

If this was so, it was a cry for help, and we had not responded to it. True, it would not have been easy — to reconcile the living with the dead, and I doubt if I would have had the courage to attempt such a task twenty-eight years ago. For this was before that extraordinary Summer of 1962, when many more amazing things were to occur.

But before revealing those events I must add a first chapter. 'A Matter of Death' is a painful necessity since it holds the key to the experiences collected under a happier title — 'And Life' —.

A MATTER OF DEATH

The world is our school and we are here to learn certain lessons. If you are a Christian, you might say the object of the exercise is to grow a little in the likeness of Christ — but there were other Teachers, just as revered, who came with the same message. Whoever or wherever we worship, the lessons are the same — there is only one God and we are on the same journey. It is a mixed school, in which people of all colours and creeds are brought together; and we must eventually learn to love one another, in the true sense of that sadly misused word.

The people we meet are our teachers, and we react to them as children do. Some we like, so we give them our attention and learn from them. Others, facing us with more difficult subjects less to our liking, invoke a different reaction. Yet it is the troublesome relationships which are of most importance. They are placed in our path, a succession of men and women who confront us with the flaws and faults in our characters. We may ignore them, escaping from the encounters bloody but unbowed, only to stumble on making the same mistakes, unhappy with ourselves and inflicting pain on others.

If we are particularly stubborn about learning our lessons it is sometimes necessary for something unfortunate or even tragic to happen, to make us face up to things and bring us to our senses. Sometimes it is only on a bed of sickness that people will lie quiet and take stock of a situation, so an illness can become a blessing in disguise. I was one of life's backward students and that was why it needed a tragedy to put me on the right path.

But before telling of the adventures which began in 1962, it is necessary to fill in the background and tell you of myself and my circumstances at that time. This gives me no more pleasure than filling out a questionnaire, or finding an old photograph of oneself one would prefer not to look at. I'll get it over as quickly as possible.

The most important thing in my childhood was an interest in the theatre. This was inevitable since my mother had attended the Royal Academy of Music with the manager of the local playhouse and he, kind man, placed a family box at her disposal. Week after week, year after year, we attended all manner of performances, and sometimes, if other theatres offered more attractive fare, we attended those also. There were also the cinema matinées to which we were accompanied by one of the servants, that they might also have 'a treat'. The amount of rubbish that passed before my eyes in those formative years must have influenced me later, for when I endeavoured to write plays they were technically sound, while firmly rooted in the trite and commonplace.

My sisters, brother and myself were all sent to good schools, and I can well believe my father's statement that the cost of our education would be the ruin of him. No one paid attention to that remark, least of all our generous mother who was never happier than when giving things away, and was quite determined that we'd have the best that money could provide. Inevitably, the crash came, and since it had never occurred to any of us that we would ever have to earn our living, we were sadly unprepared for it.

For the next thirteen years I floundered from one unsuitable job to another, holding them usually a few days, occasionally for a week, miraculously for a month, but seldom for a year. I was an impossible employee. Angry with myself for my incompetence, I hated criticism and invariably dismissed myself after a stormy, ill-tempered scene. I thought myself clever to walk out in these circumstances, mistaking my unruly temper for strength of character. I look back on the patient, long-suffering people who dealt with me and feel sorry for my treatment of them. They were, of course, my teachers, and eventually I learned that running away from difficulty was not strength, but weakness.

My only consolation during this bleak period was an amateur dramatic society formed among my friends and called, pretentiously, The Three Arts. We boasted ourselves superior to all other drama groups because we wrote, acted and produced our own plays, and we were blissfully unaware that we were terrible on all counts. The blame was surely mine since I wrote all the vehicles and listened to advice from no one.

But these amateur efforts, painful as they were to actors and audience, taught me a great deal. I learned to write dialogue and was later, in my early twenties, still writing plays when the society had long been disbanded. These were the days of the carefully plotted, well-made play, and the two top managements in the West End were HM Tennant and Linnit and Dunfee. I sent my first professional effort to the latter and received a letter inviting me to their office. Alas, they did *not* want to produce the drama. It was explained that they were also theatrical agents, and since my script was the best they'd read for some time, they'd like to represent me.

Unhappily, nothing was to come of this — I wrote several plays, but while they thought them promising, they were not produced. It took the advent of the second World War to place these set-backs in perspective. After losing all my worldly goods in the Bristol blitz I went to the General Post Office to see if there was mail for me. There was — one solitary buff envelope containing my call up papers. Granted a few weeks extension to put my affairs in order I finally arrived at a camp near Salisbury in December 1940. My welcome was as chill as the bitter winds that cut like a knife across the plain. What was I *doing* arriving at Christmas, a week before the next call up was due? The days that followed were grim indeed. Then surprisingly, I settled down and found Army life to my liking — especially two years towards the end, when stationed in North Africa.

My home-coming after the war was a sad one since my mother had sustained a major operation for cancer shortly before my arrival. It was unthinkable that I should leave her after so long an absence, yet a job would be necessary. I turned hopefully to writing. How it was possible to write comedy in those tragic circumstances, I do not know, but I managed a six part serial for the BBC's Light Programme. Mother knew it was accepted, but did not live to hear it produced.

There followed more radio scripts and a reasonably successful stage play. After this I went to America on the proceeds, to visit my eldest sister who had settled in California. I took with me a letter of introduction to a lady from the BBC who had become the director of one of the many radio stations. The hope that my English style might be marketable was quickly dashed. Her advice was that I should get any kind of employment and not attempt a script until I was 'Americanised'. Homesick and disillusioned, I used my first earnings to buy a ticket for home.

Why did I choose to settle in Windsor on my return? That, like so many things, remains a mystery. I had no friends there, no fond associations. My Uncle George had been head choir-boy at St George's Chapel in the time of Queen Victoria, but that vague connection did not influence me since I had no affection for him. I think I was torn between a love of London and the English countryside. Windsor would place me in easy reach of both.

And so, in 1954, I found myself a large shabby flat on the first floor of a Victorian house in the centre of the town. The rent, while not unreasonable was as much as I could afford, but there was a small second bedroom I could let 'if worst came to worst'. It wasn't easy, writing with the wolf at the door, so I eventually took in a lodger and came to meet the man who was to change my life completely within the next few years. While I did not know it then, this was the teacher who would at last 'get through to me' — and not before time.

Len was, at first sight, the least likely of a number of applicants. He arrived one evening on an old, well-cared for bicycle just when I was trying to decide between a schoolteacher with serious doubts about the size of the bedroom, and a sales assistant overly anxious to know if young ladies would be welcome at weekends. The possibilities of sharing the flat with either of these gentlemen seemed all too predictable, and I still hoped for an alternative. But this quiet, neatly dressed young man certainly did not appear to be the answer to my problem. Painfully shy, he seemed to direct his voice to the floor and it was almost impossible to understand a word he said. He was, in fact, apologising for having bothered me. He'd made a mistake in calling — the flat was 'far too good for him'.

This statement stopped me in my tracks. While I'd done my best with the tatty furnishings it was still the poorest apartment I'd ever lived in. My visitor was moving towards the door and since he was so painfully inarticulate, it's a wonder I didn't let him go.

'It's a bright, sunny flat,' I told him. 'But there are many things that could be done to improve it. The kitchen is small and needs shelves and cupboards —'

'I could make those —' he offered involuntarily.

'I was just making tea, so stay and have some. We can talk — but you'll have to speak up, I have trouble in understanding you. It might help if you didn't direct your voice downwards all the time.'

There I was, bossy as always, telling a timid stranger what to do, but he did not seem to resent it. The tall, stooping figure sat in an armchair and now that he raised his head I had a first good look at his pleasant, gentle face. But there was sadness in the brown eyes and premature lines about the forehead and mouth — it was a look I recognised from the faces I'd seen in the army — the look of the unwanted and underprivileged, although my interest then had been superficial.

Len had been, as I suspected, one of those unfortunates who had never had much chance in life. An unwanted child, he'd been brought up by grandparents in a Lincolnshire village. They were poor, with the added responsibility of a blind daughter, so he'd been obliged to leave school at fifteen, and sent to work in a factory some miles from home. This necessitated rising before dawn, lighting the fire and making his breakfast before cycling to work. His wage was pitifully small in those days, and all but two shillings of it were given to his benefactors. From this meagre pocket money he bought ten cigarettes which were to last him a week. Clothes were bought second-hand from market stalls.

He told me these things quite naturally. It wasn't to gain sympathy, and he wasn't being sorry for himself. He simply wanted me to appreciate the difference in our backgrounds, and why he didn't think he'd be the right one to share my flat.

'Think about it,' I said eventually. 'I'm in no great hurry. If you decide to come, I see no reason why you shouldn't be happy here.'

He had mumbled something, shaken hands and departed. I remember wondering if I'd been a bit rash. I'd been deeply touched when he told me about himself, his upbringing had been so different from mine. I'd been a spoiled brat, blissfully regardless of the Lens of this world. Surprisingly, I realised I would like to make up to him, in some small way, for all he'd missed in the past

Two days later I received a letter. The writing was impressive, each letter beautifully formed, each word carefully chosen. There was nothing here to suggest a lack of education, rather the contrary. He thanked me for my hospitality, and said he'd enjoyed our conversation. Regretfully, however, he still felt he wouldn't 'fit in' and therefore decided to remain where he was.

My first reaction was 'Well, that's that.' Then, on an impulse, I decided to go to see him. He had told me of his flat in Slough, and it was exactly as I expected; two narrow attic rooms with shared toilet facilities on the floor below. There was a minimum of furniture. Against the wall were neat stacks of carefully chosen second-hand books, and parcels of periodicals tied with cord. These were *John O'London's Weekly* - a favourite literary journal long deceased. Clearly he had spent years of solitude endeavouring to make up for his lack of education.

It was obvious he'd been considerably shaken by my unexpected visit. It had been a hot day and the flat was stifling. All I could say was 'How tidy you are.'

'There isn't much to keep tidy.'

'If I had only three things, I'd probably leave them on the floor. If you come to share my flat, I'll have to follow your good example.'

'Didn't you get my letter?'

'Of course. That's why I'm here. You can't possibly be happy in this oven — and you're paying far more rent than you need pay me.'

'What would I do with all my books?'

'Make shelves for them — you said you could do that. If I buy the wood —'

'I'd buy the wood,' he said quickly. 'I can make anything if I've a place to do it in.'

'You've a place — all you have to do is go there.'

So began an interesting experiment in human relationships, two entirely different personalities learning to live together. There were quarrels in the early days, but we accepted them as inevitable, and recognised there were lessons to be learned from such disagreements. I was used to having my own way, and thought far too much of myself, so it was for Len, in his quiet and gentle way, to take me down a peg or two.

He, on the other hand, suffered from the worst possible inferiority complex, and it was my task to help him overcome that handicap. He was so shy that it was months before he'd meet my family and friends. They, for their part, were bewildered by my choice of lodger, complaining that they could not understand a word he said. Hopefully this was something that would be corrected in time — meanwhile, I gave him the nickname 'Mumble', and this he accepted good-naturedly enough.

Len had, thank heaven, a sense of humour, and when we were alone became vivacious and amusing. It needed only a ring at the bell to send him scuttling to his room, and if it was necessary for him to meet people, he became quiet and uncommunicative again. Eventually, a few were to overcome this reserve. My sisters, on their visits to Windsor, and two old friends, Alec and Margaret Mackenzie. Shy themselves, they probably understood him better than anyone.

Clever with his hands, he transformed the flat with the aid of old tools he'd collected over the years. I had only to suggest an improvement and it was done. And when there was no more carpentry and redecorating, he took an interest in my writing, reading the scripts and correcting my atrocious spelling. Knowing my dislike for typing, he bought a second-hand machine and learned to use it. He spent hours in his room, slowly retyping pages again and again so that even a correction need not be seen. Another kindness was to tape record my radio plays, a job I never did successfully.

I tried to repay him by providing the comforts of a home and giving him small presents. The latter were accepted with almost speechless embarrassment and put away as something too good to use. He was scrupulously fair over money transactions. From the first we kept a small notebook with two columns headed 'G' and 'L' — in these we entered all we purchased in the way of food, the amounts added up and divided equally. To his share would be added his rent. He hated to owe a penny — this was something we had in common.

We also shared a love of animals. I had a tabby kitten called Bundle, and we were equally devastated when he died. Later we were to have two more tabbies, a young one called Simon, and a much older cat called Frisky. The contrasting personalities of these two caused us much amusement, and Len took many photographs of them.

The house had a garden which was far beyond the care of the elderly landlord, so Len offered to keep it in order and set aside a number of hours for that purpose. He was extremely methodical and disliked anything to disturb his routine. Friday evening was devoted to letter writing — a braille letter to his blind Aunt Dolly, another to a girl friend who lived in Lincoln. Once I was given two theatre tickets for a Friday night and was furious because he could not be persuaded to write his letters another time.

'Aunt Dolly always looks forward to my letter at the weekend.'

'It wouldn't hurt her to wait until Monday for once.'

'How do you know it wouldn't hurt? Do you know what it's like to be blind, to live alone, with only a letter to look forward to —?'

So he had gone to his little room to write his letter, and I had gone to the play, annoyed to be feeling a little ashamed of myself. I was ten years his senior, but whereas his life had made him old for his years, mine appeared to have made little impact on me — I was still, in many ways, as immature and irresponsible as a schoolboy.

But all that had been in early days. Later we were to become agreeable companions, and I honestly believe much better for the help we gave each other. A highlight in those years was a stage comedy well produced and happily received at the local Theatre Royal. I think Len enjoyed that experience as much as I, and was probably even more disappointed that it went no further after its two week run.

Yet always in the background was that dark cloud which Len had lived with so many years. He was a skilled mechanic, earning a good salary, but he hated the monotony of his work, the noise of the factory and the rough types he worked with. Week after week I would find, in his paper basket, a torn up letter he had typed, giving in his notice. One evening he told me he had made his mind up — he couldn't stand any more of it. He didn't know what his next job would be, but it wouldn't be in a factory.

This was probably the time when our roles were at last reversed. I tried to be the wise and cautious one. 'Don't you think you should get something lined up first —?'

No, he said, he'd have a break first. He felt, after all those years of doing something he hated, he deserved a long holiday, and he'd taken one — six weeks or more, partly spent with Aunt Dolly in Lincoln, but mostly around Windsor. It was a modest enough vacation spent in cycle rides exploring the countryside.

I was writing at the time something called *An Impending Disaster*. What the nonsense was about I do not remember; comedy or thriller, it was nothing of any consequence. Only the oddly prophetic title remains, for good reason, in my mind.

☆ ☆ ☆

Len finished his holiday and began his search for congenial employment, only to meet with a series of disappointments. I could see the difficulty. His intense shyness, and habit of mumbling his words when nervous, was unlikely to make a good impression at interviews, and on top of this, he was seeking work for which he had no previous experience. It was grossly unfair since he was certainly capable of other things, and was quite prepared to take a smaller salary, but no, the chance to escape was not forthcoming and finally, in desperation, he returned to the only trade he knew - at another factory in Slough.

For the following two weeks he returned too sad to even speak of his new job, and nothing I could do would cheer him. Then came a night when I woke to the sound of screaming. It seemed incredible that the noise from the next room came from my quiet gentle friend; I had never heard him shout before, but surely everyone in the house would be roused if I didn't put a stop to it. I switched on the light at the door of his room and received another shock. It might have been a stranger who lay in that dishevelled bed, bathed in perspiration, staring at me with glazed, frightened eyes. I had never been more terrified.

'I've walked into a trap —!' he shouted.

'You've been having a nightmare,' I told him, but something was already telling me it was no bad dream that had disturbed him.

My presence seemed to calm him a little, but he replied, more quietly than before 'I've walked into a trap.' The new job, I gathered, was worse than the one from which he'd escaped two months earlier.

'We'll talk about it in the morning. Try to go to sleep again —' I wiped his head with a towel and attempted to settle him down while he watched with strange, shining eyes. It was almost unbearable. There is nothing more terrible than to see a kind, familiar face suddenly transformed in this manner and to know, in your heart, that you are witnessing a mental breakdown.

He eventually slept while I sat beside his bed afraid to move my arm from behind his shoulders. Sleep, I felt, was all important. Whatever lay ahead we were to face it alone. Len's only relative — his blind Aunt Dolly — could not be expected to help. It was a grim prospect.

Then, having faced what I innocently imagined to be the worst, I prayed fervently that he'd wake up well. It was the first time I'd prayed for years. Perhaps this was why it wasn't answered, for when he woke he still had the strange look in his eyes and, when he attempted to speak, was utterly inarticulate. All his reflexes seemed in fact slower - it was necessary to help him to dress and on the short walk to the surgery he dragged his feet reluctantly. I had to explain to an elderly and strangely unsympathetic doctor, annoyed that I was unable to produce a card proving that Len was his patient. Pills were prescribed, and a visit to the hospital psychiatrist arranged.

While Len was under sedation I went to the factory to explain that he would not be returning and collect his personal tool box. A few minutes among the noise of the shop floor was enough to conjure up the nightmare poor Len had endured from the age of fifteen. And my own nightmare was only beginning.

During the days that followed living with Len grew more

and more impossible. Even under sedation he was tense and nervous, unable to sit still for a minute of the time. I recall a ball of string unravelled and rewound constantly. He could not read, listen to music or watch television; only wander restlessly from one room to another. We took long silent walks hoping they would tire him naturally, but eventually I would watch the clock for the time for taking the next pill, grateful for the blessed relief of a few hours sleep.

Then came the day when I found an electric floor plug in his room had been deliberately unscrewed and rendered dangerous, but the significance did not dawn until I later discovered a coil of rope concealed beneath his mattress. He was suicidal, and I told him he must tell the psychiatrist on his next visit, and I would go with him to be sure he'd do so.

Eventually it was for me to reveal the fact that he was attempting to take his own life, and, in the absence of relatives, had him admitted to a mental hospital. It was a ghastly thing to do, and when I left him, dazed and bewildered in the ward he pleaded piteously 'Don't leave me here — please take me with you.' I had no alternative but to turn away, and join the crowds of sad people who visited each week, hoping to find some sign of improvement.

He was discharged months later after a number of shock treatments which appeared to have made little difference. He brought with him a box of pills and was clearly as depressed as he was before entering hospital. We tried to plan for the future and talked of a job. Someone had given him the address of a government department where suitable employment was found for people recovering from mental illness. They offered him two alternatives — he could clean railway carriages or wash up dishes in an army barracks. Small wonder he returned from this interview to tell me he was 'finished'.

I had, by this time, begun to feel finished myself. Writing in this constant state of worry was impossible, and my work was being returned to me. Friends and family, gathered round, clearly concerned for both of us — I was advised to take a holiday, even if it meant Len being admitted to hospital again, but that was unthinkable, since he dreaded the place. But how long, they argued, could we hope to go on as we were?

Not long. On the evening of Friday, June the 15th 1962, I yielded to persuasion to spend an hour at the home of friends. It was to be a brief precious break from the constant watchfulness, though the worry remained with me constantly.

Someone had suggested gardening as therapy for Len and he had planted some small trees in the garden of an Old People's Home, less than a mile away. I reminded him, in a tone sharp with nerves, that he had said he would water them, so why didn't he? We had left the house at the same time, but he must have returned almost immediately, for I found him in the flat on my return. He had taken his life, but I will not distress you, or myself, with the details.

Some things, even years later, do not bear thinking about, and I would not dwell on this now if it were not necessary for the telling of the story.

It was, of course, a matter for the police, and they lost no time in answering the call. Two men made a systematic search of the small room, while a third took a statement from me, not once, but three times. The last was interrupted by one of his colleagues with a fat envelope addressed to me in Len's neat hand. They waited while I opened it, but it was not a suicide note — only three months rent in pound notes. My friend, while in no state of mind to express his feelings, had, with his customary honesty considered the sad state of my finances. It was rent in advance.

After midnight, the police locked the door of his room and departed. I spent the sleepless hours till dawn in the flat below, then announced my intention of going to Lincoln, to break the news to Aunt Dolly. My friends were against this. I was in no fit state, they said, but I was determined that the little blind lady should hear the news from me. Had anyone told me, a year before, that I could cope with it all, I would not have believed them — and neither would anyone else. *I was finding the strength.*

The strength to face the ordeal of the inquest, and retell the story of finding him before a hall filled with people who could only be there out of morbid curiosity. The strength to arrange the simple funeral. At Aunt Dolly's request, he was to be buried in Windsor. Her own parents were in the village churchyard and I think she would have liked him there, but the manner of his death was, to her mind, something to be ashamed of, and the least anyone knew, the better.

The churchyard was, it seemed appropriately, on St Leonard's Hill, and there, on a sunny June morning the man who was my friend, and certainly my teacher, was laid to rest. The nightmare, for both of us, was over.

☆ ☆ ☆

When you have lived under strain for almost a year, the relief, when the burden is finally lifted, is undeniably sweet. The sadness remained and the flat was full of memories. 'You must leave there,' advised my friends, but where could I find another place to live with a garden for my cat? Simon, my faithful tabby, had been comforting and companionable throughout the time of trouble, and I would certainly not be parted from him.

And there was another consideration. Money, or to be more accurate, the lack of it. It was a long while since I'd written or sold a script, and the idea of sharing the flat again was unthinkable. I'd have to find a job, anything at all. I was back where I was as a teenager, and no more competent at earning my living than I had been then. The verger of St George's Chapel, Windsor Castle, was advertising for a doorman. It was a task requiring little or no intelligence, the kind of thing usually offered to active pensioners, and even they seemed reluctant to accept the long hours, and the small wage. So I pocketed my pride and secured the humble post, in the face of absolutely no competition. No one wanted the job but me.

AND LIFE

1

It was a week after the funeral that I had the first strange experience. I had woken before dawn and lay, fully awake, watching the sky grow lighter and listening to the birds. I stress the fact that I was in this state for fully an hour, calm and at peace with myself. And then the voice had spoken to me, so clearly that I would have thought anyone, even outside the door, could have heard it. It spoke five words: '*He did it for you.*'

There was nothing frightening about it, and I know now that the voice was on 'the inner ear' and would not, therefore, have been heard by others. Greatly wondering, I repeated the words over and over in order not to forget them. They must, of course, refer to Len, and the unknown speaker presumably wished me to know why he died as he did. Later, when I discussed the matter with the Mackenzies, they agreed the words made sense to them. They had visited Len and heard him say, more than once, how concerned he was to be such a burden to me. But what were the alternatives? A blind aunt could not cope, and the thought of returning to the mental hospital horrified him.

On mentioning the hearing of the voice I saw an anxious glance exchanged between my two friends. I'd stood up to things so well -was I breaking now, when the worst was over?

It was not in my nature to dismiss the incident. I knew the voice had not been a figment of my imagination, so somehow it had to be accounted for. The only place where I felt I might seek an answer was in a Spiritualist Church. There were two in Windsor, and I chose the Sanctuary of St John the Divine, hidden away in an old house behind a shop in the High Street.

It is perhaps important that I should state at this point my attitude towards Spiritualism at this time. It was that which was considered healthy and normal among most men and women; extreme scepticism, laced with an indulgent amusement. My idea of a medium was probably personified by the late Hermione Gingold, who, in one of the *Gate Revues,* stalked the stage in grotesque make-up singing: 'I'm only a medium medium, and my fees are exceedingly small.' One wonders who the unfortunate lady was on whom she modelled her caricature.

Then there was *Blithe Spirit* and the absurdly lovable Madame Arcarti. Was Noel Coward aware of the truth of Spiritualism when writing that delightful comedy? I know now that there was nothing there which could not have been the truth, exaggerated and 'played for laughs'. But certainly in the summer of 1962 I was serious minded, sceptical, by no means gullible, and therefore able to examine the things that happened analytically. It was this sane, scientific approach which was to lead me later to an understanding of religion in the true sense.

Over the door was written: *All Seekers after the Truth are welcome here.* It was Sunday evening and the service due to commence at seven. The Sanctuary had been a large upstairs drawing room, and the atmosphere of peace and tranquility enfolded all who entered. There was an altar with a large brass cross and vases of flowers. An upright piano. Seven rows of dining room chairs, and long windows overlooking a garden. But it was almost time for the service to begin, and no sign of life in that silent house.

I sat in the back row and waited. Eventually a lady arrived and sat in the second row, then an elderly couple who settled half-way back. A clock on the mantel piece chimed the hour. We waited, a congregation of four. Five minutes later there were stirrings in the house, footsteps on the stairs, a rustling of silk. Two ladies entered, the first tall and elderly, the second small and younger. They smiled upon us, apparently undismayed that we were few in number.

The tall lady welcomed us with the assurance that while we were few 'in the flesh' they *knew* the sanctuary was just full of souls who had gathered there. 'And I know we will have a beautiful service because it will be taken by our dear Elsie Cripps.' Having made the introduction she sat on the piano stool, and it was her friend who announced the hymn.

It was, to all appearances, an orthodox service. A hymn, the Lord's Prayer, a reading from the Bible and a further hymn. The address, since I was unfamiliar with trance mediumship, puzzled me considerably. Miss Cripps, her eyes tightly closed, appeared to be speaking in a voice quite unlike her own. It was a pious sermon and went on a very long time.

During the singing of a third hymn, announced by the lady at the piano, the medium fumbled her way into a chair by the altar and eventually opened her eyes. The clock chimed eight. Surely the service would soon draw to a close? But no - Miss Cripps rose from her chair and to my great astonishment pointed in my direction.

'I'm drawn to the gentleman in the back row -'

'Me -?' I gasped, absurdly, since there was no one else.

'I have your mother with you. Let me describe her. She is slight of build, about your own height. Her hair is white. She tells me it became so quite early in life - it didn't bother her - and it grows *nicely* - do you know what I mean by this? She has what they call a 'widow's peak'. Her eyes are blue. Blue-grey might be a better description - she is wearing blue and I feel if she did so her eyes would seem of the same colour -'.

That was exactly true - she was describing my mother far better than I, at short notice, could do myself.

'Your mother is telling me you have recently been involved in a most grievous tragedy. She could not prevent this happening, only give you the strength to stand up to it -

'*The strength to stand up to it* -'. How well I could believe that since I'd never understood the courage that possessed me at the time.

The message ended with the assurance of her love for me. It was utterly convincing. I sat in dazed silence, oblivious that Miss Cripps was now delivering messages to others, and I would have liked, if it had been possible, to slip quietly away. After a further hymn and a final blessing, the service ended. The medium, looking understandably exhausted, left the room while the other lady came to introduce herself.

Her name was Mrs Crispe. They hadn't seen me there before. Had I enjoyed the service? Did I realise who had spoken through Elsie? They knew him as the Shepherd of the Hills, a dear soul who'd lived at the time of Christ. And what did I think of my message? Wasn't it wonderful that my mother had come through to me -?

I agreed it was wonderful and told her I wanted to go away, just to think about it. She was a beautiful old lady with bright brown eyes and an Edwardian hour-glass figure. The fact that I had never before attended such a service had not occurred to her, and she was able to recall every word of my message. She was sympathetic about the tragedy. 'You must pray for that dear soul - people who go over in such circumstances find it difficult -.'

So I began my prayers, and since my mother knew all about it, I asked that she and my father would be parents to Len. This was something he'd always wanted and never had — but it seemed there was another world in which such things were possible.

☆ ☆ ☆

My friends were vaguely alarmed by my sudden interest in Spiritualism. They had to admit the message was surprising, but wasn't it possible the medium was reading my mind?

'But I wasn't even thinking of my mother,' I argued.

'You may not have been *thinking* of her, but your knowledge of her appearance was in your head somewhere. You *could* have described her.'

'Not as accurately as she did. And how did she know of the tragedy?'

'It was in the paper less than a fortnight ago.'

'But even if they'd read about it, they weren't likely to connect it with me.' I was becoming quite angry. 'It's absurd to suggest the medium isn't genuine. How about her trance address?'

'She could be a frustrated actress.'

'She'd have to be *very* frustrated to learn a forty minute speech to perform for an audience of four.'

There were a dozen people the following Sunday. Perhaps a change in the weather was responsible. Elsie was entranced on this occasion, not by a Biblical character but a very different personality who spoke in a high, querulous voice. The theme was clearly the Responsibility of Writers. There were those in the realms of Spirit who were very concerned about the quality of the written word upon the earthplane. They deplored the emphasis on sex and violence and wondered if the authors had any conception of the harm they did? The speaker had come to urge and implore a change in their standards. What the world needed desperately were books and plays of an uplifting nature.

When message time arrived I was almost passed by. There were 'lights around me, many doors opening'. That was all, and should have been enough, but I'd hoped for more.

'Wasn't that a wonderful address?' enthused Mrs Crispe before anyone but Elsie had time to leave. 'I'm wondering who it was meant for? Are any of you writers, by any chance?'

I, who had never typed an uplifting word, admitted somewhat sheepishly that I had written a few things.

'Then it was for you,' she said. 'It's really quite extraordinary how the address seems to be given especially for a newcomer to our Sanctuary. I'm sure it was helpful.'

It had been thought-provoking, certainly, but while sex and violence had never been my stock-in-trade I could not see myself earning my living with writing of a loftier nature.

The following Sunday Elsie's trance address purported to come from the Most Rev William Temple. It was certainly powerful and impressive, but it was her message to me afterwards that really amazed me.

'I have two people here beside you, a man and wife. They are country folk, and the man tells me he worked on the land. They lived near Stamford, Lincoln. They've come to thank you for what you tried to do for the boy, and for breaking the news to their daughter.' Elsie paused, frowning. 'I've been asking who they are, but I only get the wife's name. It's Lily.'

But they were giving their surname. These were Len's grandparents, for his aunt's name was Dorothy Lilley.

☆ ☆ ☆

It was only natural I should want to tell Aunt Dolly this wonderful proof of survival. I had promised to write to her anyway, in a small attempt to fill the gap left by Len's weekly letter. But my letters would have to be read by a neighbour, and, knowing her reticence, I could not disclose matters of such a personal and private nature.

The only answer was to find someone with a braille typewriter who would undertake the work for a small fee. The Blind Association gave me the address of a Mr Brown who lived in a terraced house not far from the cemetery. I decided to go and see him as soon as the letter was written.

To ease the boredom of my job as doorman, I had provided myself with a pocket notebook in which to record an occasional snatch of interesting conversation or amusing incident. They were few and far between, but now the little book really came in useful as I noted down the extraordinary happenings which had so confounded me, and might surely bring some consolation to anyone left desolate through the loss of a loved one.

It was, as you may imagine, no easy task. I had no wish to frighten Aunt Dolly, and since she was a simple soul, living alone in perpetual darkness, there was this possibility. But the events of the past few weeks had certainly taken the edge off my grief, and if I recounted them quite simply, thinking them over would surely be better than the knowledge that she was now quite alone.

The Browns, when I met them, were more than happy to co-operate. The good man, totally blind, showed me with pride his braille typewriter, and his wife agreed to read the letter at dictation speed. There was to be no question of payment - they were more than happy to be of service, for surely the blind should help the blind? I noticed, while we talked in their living room, a Methodist hymn book on their piano, and they were interested to know that the lady to whom they would be writing was also a Methodist We parted on the happiest of terms.

They must have read the letter that evening, for two days later I received a disappointing little note from Mrs Brown.

She said they were sorry, but when she read what I had written she and her husband had decided that they could not be party to passing on such information. They were Methodists and prayed directly to God. Their reluctance should not have surprised me, knowing the air of suspicion that surrounded anything to do with Spiritualism. I wrote back and said I was sorry they felt as they did, but thought perhaps they had the wrong idea of Spiritualists since the ones I had met were sincerely religious and also prayed to God. I thought this was probably the end of the matter, and did not mention it to anyone.

The following Sunday I went to the afternoon service at the Sanctuary. This was at three, and conducted by a Mr Wilfred Collis while Elsie rested in readiness for the evening. Mrs Crispe and I were the only other people present and it was the formula as before, mainly interesting from the point of watching a male medium at work. I barely knew this gentleman and was wondering if he would give clairvoyance, when he suddenly spoke to me.

'I have your mother with you - she's saying you must not be disappointed if people do not believe as you do. Do you understand why she should say that?'

In view of what had happened, I did. Mr Collis seemed to be listening intently, then added. 'She has said something else which I do not understand but must repeat to you. She says 'The gentleman *will* write the letter, but not yet, for he's ill in bed with a fever'. Do you understand that?'

I certainly did not.

'Then remember it, will you? I haven't been able to hold her, but it obviously means something or she would not have given it.'

The mystery was accounted for a few days later on a postcard which is now before me. It was written by Mrs Brown on behalf of her husband.

14.8.62

Dear Mr Adams,
So pleased to have your letter, which throws new light on the situation.
Unfortunately, I have been in bed, with a temperature,

since last Thursday, but will tackle the braille as soon as I'm about again.

Yours sincerely,

Leslie Brown

No mind-reading was involved here, and even the most sceptical of my friends were unable to account for it. My explanation is a simple one. Mother was with me when I delivered the letter, and remained as a matter of interest to note the Browns' reaction to it. With her lively and inquisitive mind it is exactly what she would have done during her lifetime, and the incident seemed conclusive proof that she was still very much alive on another level of consciousness.

2

During the weeks that followed I became a frequent visitor to the house in the High Street, and the help I received there was immeasurable. Constance Crispe was a remarkable woman who had first discovered Spirit communication through friends on a purely superficial level. Since she had deep religious convictions, she decided this was not good enough. As far as she was concerned, mediumship should only be used for a higher purpose. If it was possible to contact friends and relatives in Spirit realms, then there were surely wonderful, learned souls who could give us the benefit of the far greater wisdom they had received on 'the other side of life'.

After spending many days and nights in prayer, she had the courage to turn her drawing-room into a sanctuary, and open the door of her house to the public. There must have been many times in the early days when things were difficult, for she needed the help and support of like-minded people. More importantly, a medium *worthy* of the great souls. Only a 'pure vessel' would do, a man or woman as devout and dedicated as she was herself.

Elsie Cripps, she was convinced, came to her in answer to her prayers, and certainly that remarkable little woman fulfilled her highest hopes. I lost count of the great souls who used her, twice a week. as a channel for their long, earnest sermons. This was in 1962. How long Elsie had been 'used' before then, I do not know, but she still continues to be of service at the time of writing.

The trouble was that Mrs Crispe, having set this high standard, was now finding it difficult to acquire those 'seekers after the truth' that were so welcome to join them. She was determined that while clairvoyance would be part of the service, the congregation would not receive messages from loved ones until they'd spent some time in prayer, and listened to a long address. Fair enough. There were the faithful few who were happy with this arrangement, but they *were* few. I counted myself fortunate to be one of them.

Dora Middleton travelled quite a distance to attend an occasional service - a long and trying journey by bus and train, involving a great deal of time and considerable expense. The latter must have been an important factor, for she was the poorly paid cook-housekeeper of a cantankerous and miserly old lady.

'Enough to try the patience of a saint,' said Elsie.

'Why does she put up with her, if she's so nasty?' I asked practically.

'Because she's a sick woman. Dora feels sorry for her. She's a very lovely soul.'

Dora's plain little face, devoid of make-up, certainly radiated a cheerful good nature, and I liked her instinctively. When it came to message time, I listened unashamed to hear what she was told.

'Little Mother,' sighed the entranced Elsie, taking her hand. 'I don't have to tell you how highly you are regarded in the realms of spirit. There are many here who are aware of the wonderful work you do with those little ones - and one who would advise you -'

There followed a great deal of detailed advice, given in a totally different voice, and many children were named. Dora understood perfectly, asked and answered questions, and was obviously grateful for this lengthy discourse. I was told afterwards that she did invaluable work in her sleep state, helping children and babies who had passed through acts of violence or accidents. At this stage of experience I was unable to comprehend this, and could only listen in amazement.

☆ ☆ ☆

One Sunday, the entranced Elsie delivered a particularly powerful address which, like many others, appeared to go on for a very long time. Again, a different voice but I could see, from the first utterance, that Constance Crispe was excited by it. She hurried to switch on the tape recorder, which, for reasons of economy, was not always used.

'William Temple,' she told us afterwards. 'It's not often he honours us with his presence.'

'Is *that* who it was?' asked Elsie. 'I did wonder. I knew it was a very powerful soul, for I felt lifted right up.'

I had noticed, when she came out of her trance, that she appeared dazed and bewildered, as if afraid to take a step in case of falling from a height. It always took a few minutes before she became her normal self again.

'He's left me very tired,' she added.

(The Most Reverend William Temple was Archbishop of Canterbury from 1942 until the time of his death in 1944. An outstanding Christian leader whose influence was felt among people of all denominations. Incidentally, I was told that when a taped address given through Elsie was played to clergymen who had known him personally, they bore witness to the fact that it was indeed the voice, and style, of that great preacher.)

On Sundays I would attend both afternoon and evening services, and the three hours between the two were spent with Mrs Crispe, Wilfred Collis, and occasionally Elsie. Sometimes we were joined by a visitor who would have attended the afternoon session or come some distance to be present later. We'd have an old-fashioned tea round the table in one of the smaller downstairs rooms, and this was my opportunity to learn a great deal. While I was now convinced of Spirit communication, there were still many things I was sceptical about. They were splendidly open-minded about this.

'It's the way we want you to be. Don't believe all you're told, don't believe all you read. Question everything.'

'And pray for answers,' Mrs Crispe would say. 'That's what I was told to do in the early days. If there's anything you don't understand, pray to be shown. The answer will come.'

But Constance Crispe, wise and loving as she was, could be autocratic. I once asked to be told something about ghosts.

'*Spirits!*' she said quite sharply. 'They're *Spirits,* not ghosts! You wouldn't want to be called a ghost, would you?'

'No,' I admitted.

'They're just the same as you are only you happen to be in a physical body.'

I recalled what someone had told me earlier. Most people think of themselves only as a physical body with something vague, which might be described as their Spirit. But if they think like this they have their priorities wrong, for they are first and foremost Spirit, and their body the lesser part, to be eventually discarded like a worn-out garment.

On another occasion we discussed Spiritual Healing. This was an important part of their ministry and one evening a week was set aside for it. I had been advised to attend for a few weeks, for I'd lost a lot of weight and felt very depleted when first attending the Sanctuary. Someone remarked that I looked better and hoped I was completely well.

'I'm fine,' I told them 'But I still seem to run temperatures now and again.'

'*Temperatures -?*'

'Well, yes, I wouldn't know how else to describe them. I just feel suddenly warm for no reason at all.'

This seems to cause some amusement.

'*Temperatures!* You aren't running temperatures - you feel like that when the Spirit friends come close.'

I was about to question this statement when I recalled the last times I'd experienced the warm feelings. The first was on visiting the Browns, and the second when Wilfred had given me the last message from my mother that Sunday afternoon.

All the people around the tea table seemed to have shared the warm glow, and it was a relief to know I wasn't sickening for something, particularly since the running of 'temperatures' had recurred at intervals all my life.

But nobody mentioned, that afternoon, the reverse side of the 'warm glow' - the ghastly chill which creeps up on you when in the presence of an evil entity. This I was to experience when helping to exorcise a badly haunted house, but that event comes much later - far more pleasant things were to happen first.

☆ ☆ ☆

Messages, and more messages - but not the one I was hoping for. Then came a communication from a monk who wanted me to know that my prayers were helping my friend. That was all, and reassuring as it was I had hoped for more.

'You can't possibly expect to hear from him yet,' I was told. 'You must learn to be patient.'

Meanwhile, I heard of guides and helpers, of which I appeared to have quite a number. Then, one evening when Elsie paused before me, she appeared to see and hear something which pleased her enormously.

'There's such joy and excitement around you, such plans for your future! They're taking you away from your present employment and finding something more to your liking. They want you to start writing again. And they're also planning a new place for you to live. Somewhere where you'll have no rent to pay. What's more, there'll be a garden for your cat.'

It all sounded so fantastic, ridiculous and unbelievable. I had the greatest respect for Elsie's mediumship but felt, on this particular evening, that something had gone wrong somewhere. Could it be that some imp of mischief had crept in?

I'm afraid I made fun of it, and so did my friends. It became quite a joke as weeks went by. 'You haven't your rent-free flat, then?'

'Not yet,' I would say. 'But I live in hope. It was all a bit naughty and I would not have dared to make fun of the message before Mrs Crispe, Elsie, or any of their intimates.

Then, when the joke had worn so thin as to be almost forgotten, another message arrived on the same theme.

'Your loved ones in Spirit are so excited. Their plans for you are almost completed. They're showing me the house where you'll live. It's large, Victorian — approached by a drive.

'It stands in its own grounds with a big garden. There are steps leading to a red front door. I see the door opening and a lady welcoming you in. You follow her into a square, high-ceilinged room on the left of the hall. There's an open log fire. The lady sits on the settee, and you sit opposite. There's a piece of furniture beside you, but I can't see what it is — only that it's covered with bright, shiny objects that flicker in the firelight.'

Dear Elsie, I thought, off on another flight of fancy, but I noted it down as quickly as possible.

Two weeks later I stood at the window of my flat looking down on the garden. Simon, never far from my side, sat on the window seat and I was suddenly aware that there was something below that excited him, and he wished to draw my attention to it. It was a Siamese cat, and while I was familiar with most of the local felines, this handsome creature was new to me. Probably lost, I thought, and shutting Simon in the room, for fear of repercussions. I hurried down to investigate, hoping he'd still be there when I arrived. Not only was he there, but he came and sat at my feet, looking up at me with incredible blue eyes.

While I love all the cat family, Siamese are a breed I'm not familiar with, and am therefore a little wary of, but he allowed me to pick him up without a murmur of protest, and read the name and address on his smart green collar. The owner's name was Hewitt and the house only a short distance down the next road.

Mr Hewitt and his wife were delighted to have their cat returned to them. Surprised, however, that he'd strayed from their own large garden, and somewhat astonished that he'd allowed me to pick him up. They invited me to join them in a glass of sherry. We talked. So I also had a cat? Yes, they had seen the big handsome tabby that sat on the gatepost of the corner house. And what did I do -?

I hesitated to say that I stood at the back door of St George's Chapel, for no better purpose than to prevent people from entering without paying at the front. Instead, I admitted to being a writer down on his luck, doing temporary work just to keep going. Mrs Hewitt, herself a novelist, was sympathetic and eased the situation by saying she'd enjoyed my comedy at the Theatre Royal.

'I have a bookshop by the bridge into Eton,' said her husband diffidently. 'You wouldn't care to be my assistant?'

I cared. A job 'more to my liking' had been found.

☆ ☆ ☆

Arthur Hewitt was a good, kind man with the patience of a saint. We each kept our own book and till, and at the end of the day, when he had balanced his, it was usually necessary to help me with mine. I tried to be extra helpful in other ways to compensate for my hopelessness at figures, and we seemed to get along in spite of this handicap.

'There's something I've been meaning to ask you, Gyles,' he said one evening a few weeks after employing me. 'Would you happen to know of a woman who'd like a rent-free flat? My wife and I are trying to help a friend who is looking for someone. She has a flatlet house here in Windsor, but she's recently divorced her husband and feels too unhappy to remain there. The idea is to find someone who'll live on the premises and collect the rents. It's her own flat - five lovely ground floor rooms and a garden -' he broke off suddenly 'But you know, this doesn't have to be a woman. Wouldn't you like to consider it? You can't really be happy living where you are, after what happened there.'

I gasped and said 'Yes, I would.' Since he didn't know of Elsie's prediction, he couldn't realize how overwhelming his words had been.

'I'll talk to my wife this evening. I'm sure she'll think it an excellent idea. Then we'll phone Cissie and put it to her.'

It was arranged that I should call on the lady next day. And there, at the end of a short drive, was the square, Victorian house with the red front door. Cissie, who I'd never seen in my life before, opened the door as I mounted the steps.

'I've already decided that you're the one for my flat.' she said. Clearly the Hewitts had given a good account of me.

We entered the hall and turned left into a lovely, high-ceilinged room. A log fire burned in the big open grate. Cissie waved me to an armchair while settling down on the settee. She was a tall elegant lady with sad eyes, but there were other things on my mind at that moment.

There was, at my side, a curious piece of furniture composed of three shelves. On these were the lady's collection of old glass paper-weights, and they flickered in the firelight as described by Elsie in her 'flight of fancy' I'd ridiculed a few weeks earlier.

The notebook in which I recorded my 'psychic messages' was in my inside pocket, and I decided, on an impulse, to produce it and share the wonder of the moment. Cissie was amazed and bewildered at the accurate description of what had just happened, and it was some time before we could settle down to business.

She had bought a house in another part of the country, and was eager to hand over as soon as possible. All she wanted me to do was collect the rents every month, and pay the cheques into her account. Her daily woman would continue to clean the house and my own flat as well. She also wanted me to keep the phone, at her expense, in case it was ever necessary to call her.

So Simon and I moved in a month later, and the new job and new home became a reality. There were minor problems. While Cissie had kindly left fitted carpets and curtains, it was up to me to furnish the large rooms. Since my luck seemed to be changing, I bought a suite, bed and wardrobe on instalments. The garden was to remain a problem since I could not cope with it, but Simon liked it just the way it was, and soon made it his personal jungle. We settled down to our new life in a surprisingly short space of time.

3

There were many reasons for me to feel happier, and the interesting new job and pleasant rent-free flat were only two of them. Now that I'd left the scene of the tragedy, the memory began to recede a little, and this was helped by the fact that there were many new things demanding attention. I felt no urge to write as yet, but that was not important now that my finances no longer depended on it. Instinct told me that when I did write again it would be something very different from the comedies and thrillers of the past This was not due to that sobering address on a writer's responsibility. I knew myself changed and the desire simply to entertain was no longer enough.

Truly I was making a new start in life on both material and spiritual levels, but it was the latter that was responsible for the deep joy and sense of excitement. After the events already described my feelings at this time can hardly be wondered at. I felt like someone facing up to mysteries far more complex than any I'd invented in the past It was little wonder that the people at the Sanctuary were so important to me. Who else would understand, or endeavour to explain?

Mother had 'died' in 1945, yet returned in my time of need in 1962. She had 'given me the strength' to stand up to my troubles, and this I can firmly believe since I knew this strength was beyond my own resources. Yet how does a Spirit from the past give strength to one in the present? Perhaps it is the time element that confuses us here, for time is a very complex thing. Invented by man for use on the earth plane, we have become slaves to it, but there are those who say the past, present and future are one, and this may explain the seemingly unexplainable.

This is admittedly beyond my understanding, yet I see something in the theory. How was Elsie able to describe, in precise detail, my visit to the house weeks later? Was it prophecy, or was she seeing the actual event? Perhaps that is the explanation of prophecy. I have not the knowledge to engage in weighty theological speculation, and if I appear to be floundering, make no apology. I'm sharing my ideas with you for your own consideration. I don't know the answers, and doubt if you do. It's as if, at the moment, we see just a corner of a gigantic painting, or stand with a piece of jigsaw in our hand. We may glimpse a little more of the canvas, or anticipate the next piece of the puzzle, but we'll never really know until the whole picture is revealed to us.

As for my mother's intervention — it helps to realize we are *both Spirits*. So if you forget my physical body it is easier to understand that she dealt with my *spirit*, possibly while I slept, and it was that part of me which upheld the physical in the time of adversity.

'They find ways of helping us,' said Mrs Crispe, and I could not doubt this, remembering the 'plans for the future'. Arthur Hewitt had wanted an assistant, and Cissie needed someone for her flat. Had they prayed for the answers to their problems, or were they in the hands of guardian angels who knew their needs, and got together with mine? It sounds frivolous, expressed like that, but it certainly looked as if Spirit friends took an interest in our affairs and were able to manipulate them. It made one feel as if secret agents were at work in our lives, but if their activities were for our good we could only be grateful.

Even the manner in which the plan was made to operate gave me cause to wonder. Simon at the window, drawing my attention to the Siamese cat in the garden. And even the behaviour of the Siamese had contributed strangely to the enterprise. Am I suggesting, then, that cats were used to further the plan? Why not? If Spirit friends were able to bring people together in the right place at the right time, then surely they could influence animals?

I recalled, with a thrill of excitement, an incident during

Len's lifetime. I had finished typing my stage comedy and sat with the script before me, wondering what on earth I was to do with it. Suddenly I remembered that Simon, our newly acquired kitten, was down in the garden, and while it was protected from the road by a high wall, it must have been nearly an hour since I'd left him there. At first I saw no sign of him, then located the small striped body at the back of a flower bed. He was obviously trying to get through the fence to the next garden.

This had struck me at the time as odd behaviour on the part of a kitten. There was nothing of special interest in the garden of Number Two, and since the owners of the house disliked cats and had a son who shot at them with an air rifle, I hurried down to retrieve him.

By the time I arrived he had crossed the forbidden territory and was now attempting to negotiate the neat fence that divided that garden from the lawn and flower beds of Number Three. I knew this house was owned by Ruth Goddard, an actress I had often admired on the stage but never met. When I sneaked through the side door, hoping to fetch the trespasser unknown to anyone, the lady had come out to greet him and was standing with Simon in her hands.

So it could be said that my kitten introduced us, and as a result Ruth and her actress daughter Phoebe Kershaw read my play and liked it sufficiently to show it to John Counsell, the artistic director of the Theatre Royal. He had always liked the idea of producing something by a local writer, and the comedy was presented soon after. None of this would have happened if it hadn't been for Simon, who I now referred to as 'my agent with the fur coat'.

The fact that this story bears a strong resemblance to the circumstances that led to my introduction to the Hewitts, can hardly be coincidental; cats 'did the honours' on both occasions, and the results were certainly to my advantage. Incidentally, there's been a time since when another cat was the means of doing me a good turn. It's all too easy to say they 'bring me luck', there must be more to it than that.

Since this is to be not only a record of experiences but also an investigation into Spiritualism, it may be appropriate to say that it is only in recent years that the movement has been made respectable, and officially recognized as a religion. Bertha Harris, a veteran medium, recalled the early struggles — meetings held in small halls that were sometimes raided by the police. The indignity of being taken to the station, and even detained in the cells. But it wasn't very long before that, that sensitives suffered even more for their psychic gifts, and were burned as witches!

There are now Spiritualist churches in most large towns - sometimes more than one, since there are two kinds. There are the Christian Spiritualist churches and those of the National Spiritualist Union. The main function of both is to prove survival, and having done so, to impress upon people the importance of living a worthwhile life here in preparation for the next.

The Christian Spiritualists acknowledge the divinity of Christ, place a cross on the altar, read from the Bible and adhere to its teaching. The National Spiritualist Union replace the altar with a platform, and the cross with a picture of Christ, claiming he was a great prophet, teacher and healer, but not necessarily divine. They read from their own version of the Bible, *The Aquarian Gospel*, or any other book considered of a spiritual nature.

Both churches need mediums for the clairvoyance at the end of the service, and usually these hard-worked individuals give the intercession, reading and address as well. So the quality of the service stands and falls on the ability of the sensitive, and while this country appears to have an abundance of psychics, there are clearly not enough good ones to go round. It is also worth remembering that they are seldom paid more than the minimum travelling expenses, so that they not only give up a Sunday to their work but are frequently out of pocket as well.

The Sanctuary of St John the Divine was unique in every respect. Elsie Cripps was its resident medium. This meant that you always knew the standard to expect, and if the visitor found the service 'too high' for their taste, they went to the other. Curious to know what the opposition was like, but knowing Mrs Crispe would not approve, I went along to a mid-week service.

The little church at Adelaide Square held about a hundred, and was already half-full fifteen minutes before the service was due to begin. Members of the congregation had been buying their *Psychic News* at the door, and either sat reading or chatting to their neighbour. Constance Crispe would have been horrified. Only recently she had heard two ladies holding a whispered conversation in the Sanctuary, and sternly drawn their attention to the notice requesting silence. Since I loved to sit and meditate, I appreciated her attitude, but it was also easy to understand why the attendance was so small.

The Adelaide Square service, conducted by the President, Mrs Kittie Simpson, was bright, happy and certainly evidential, but the messages received were shorter and far more 'down to earth' than those delivered by Elsie at the Sanctuary. There was good reason for this — Mrs Simpson addressed herself to at least a dozen people, whereas Elsie, dealing with smaller numbers, could spend more time with each individual. Her communications were therefore of a deeper, more spiritual nature. But we should not dismiss the messages given in Spiritualist Churches as trite and superficial. They may sound so to everyone but the person who receives them. I was told: 'You have a man with you who tells me he taught you how to wash your face.' That must have sounded ridiculous to the rest of the people present, but I placed him immediately, even though he was someone I hadn't thought of for years.

Many years before, I had had my portrait painted by an Australian artist, Leonard James Green. This was not out of vanity - it had been one of my 'odd jobs'. I'd been paid by the hour, and the sittings had lasted several weeks. He was, I imagined, a man in his early thirties, with hardly a line on his healthy, boyish face. When he told me he was far older than he looked, he said the reason was that he never used a face flannel - just soap and water - massaging the skin with his fingertips. I adopted this method ever after, so you can see why that brief message brought instant recall.

Kittie Simpson is a minister of the Spiritualist Church which means she can conduct weddings, naming ceremonies and funerals. A 'naming ceremony', the equivalent to a Christening, has one important difference.

Spiritualists do not go along with the use of water 'to wash away sin' and the baby is scattered with flower petals instead. Funerals are cheerful affairs. Having attended one conducted by this lady I told her 'I'd like you to take the service for me, when my time comes,' whereupon she whipped out her diary and asked 'What date had you in mind, dear?'

This caused much laughter and underlines an important truth. True spiritualists are unafraid of death. But I would not say they were alone in this. It is not death itself but the manner of dying that daunts people. Yet I firmly believe we are given the strength to bear whatever comes our way.

The Adelaide Square church had much to recommend it, but I knew in my heart the Sanctuary would always be my choice. In my time of trouble I may well have found kindness, but not the consolation in that more popular church. To begin with, the sheer number of people would have frightened me away.

There was no doubt that the house in the High Street had become a sanctuary in the true sense of the word. It was not merely that I liked the people and learned from them, it seemed that religion had at last become meaningful under their roof. It was a joy to go there - and this made the following incident all the stranger.

I had approached the house as usual, some minutes before seven on a Sunday evening, feeling happy, even exhilarated. It was not just the anticipation of the meeting with friends and the possibility of a 'message'. I wanted to pray and give thanks for all that had been revealed to me.

Then, as I stretched out my hand to turn the doorknob, it was suddenly arrested in mid-air. It was not a sudden seizure or paralysis. My hand and arm felt perfectly normal. It was simply as if an invisible barrier had come down about a foot in front of me. I tried again and it was still impossible. It would seem I was up against a screen of glass, or ice, since it was intensely cold. Bewildered and a little frightened, I turned away, and walked about Windsor, baffled and unhappy.

I called next day to explain my absence, but it was scarcely necessary. When they did not find me in the Sanctuary, they knew what was happening. 'When those in darkness see someone accepting Christ they do everything in their power to prevent them,' said Mrs Crispe. 'What you experienced last evening was the force of evil. We prayed for you, and feel the crisis is past'

☆ ☆ ☆

Further evidence of the 'force of evil' was brought to us next Sunday afternoon. Mrs Crispe, Wilfred and I were about to start when we were joined by the roughest, toughest type of man I'd ever seen in any church. He was of medium height, stockily built, and wore motor-cycle gear. He strode in, sat himself in the third row, and proceeded to tuck a garish crash helmet under his seat. He then removed his leather jacket and hung it on the back of the chair in front. His shirt sleeves were rolled up to his elbows and his arms were decorated with elaborate tattoos, but I noticed he did not loosen the grubby white scarf about his neck.

To give him his due, he sat through the entire service, though I fully expected him to leave during the long address. He made no attempt to join in the singing of the hymns, and when the time came for clairvoyance I was startled to hear Wilfred say: 'I don't have to tell you — you are no stranger to all this?'

The young man grunted in the affirmative. Could it really be that this unlikely character was in the habit of attending Spiritualist churches?

But no, as I listened unashamedly to more of the message, it dawned on me that the man was psychic. Wilfred was saying he had a natural gift and should develop it to benefit mankind. He didn't look the least interested. If he'd come for a message it wasn't one of a spiritual nature.

Mrs Crispe, who must have been burning with curiosity, spoke to him afterwards. 'May I ask what brought you here this afternoon?' she inquired, with her customary directness. He didn't mind telling her. In fact he'd come to unburden himself, and told a hair-raising story.

Yes, it was true he was psychic. He'd been able to see spirit people 'since he was a nipper' - see, but not hear them - and the night before he had 'heard' for the first time.

Some friends had recently taken over an old inn not far from the castle. (We knew it as one which had long had an unsavoury reputation) He'd been given a small upstairs room and awakened in the night to a long, terrifying scream. When he opened his eyes he saw, beside the bed, the spirit form of 'a wild looking woman with blazing eyes' intent on harming him.

'Didn't you call upon the Lord?' asked the old lady mildly.

He was about to say 'You bet I bloody well did', but managed to modify the statement for her delicate ears.

'And she went away,' said she, with a gentle smile. 'Dear boy, you realize that poor soul could not really have harmed you?'

'Oh, no -?' said the dear boy, loosening the scarf about his neck. 'How about this, then -?'

There were certainly some ugly red marks on his throat and she blinked in surprise on seeing them. 'She wouldn't have had the strength to strangle you,' she asserted.

Naturally, we discussed the matter at tea time. It had all come as a great revelation to me, proving in the first instance that psychic gifts were not necessarily the prerogative of people like Wilfred and Elsie.

'Indeed not,' said Elsie 'Gypsies that tell fortunes are probably employing a psychic gift, but you'd hardly call them spiritual.'

'I can't get over the marks on his throat,' I said.

'Spirit people can move things from one place to another, so we know they have strength,' Mrs Crispe explained 'But I still say she couldn't have killed him.'

'She wouldn't have needed to lay hands on me' I told them. 'I'd have died of fright long before then.'

'It wouldn't have happened to you. Another type of man - or a woman - could sleep in that room and nothing would happen. *Like attracts like* - always remember that. That woman was probably a prostitute, murdered by such a man, and when his counterpart stays there, he draws her into the conditions. Being psychic, he was aware of her.'

'She certainly terrified him.'

'Not sufficiently to induce him to change his ways. I doubt if we'll ever see him again.'

Would she have wanted him visiting the Sanctuary? Possibly not, but I think all those good people would have given him the benefit of private counselling, had he been prepared to receive it. But 'you cannot sow seeds unless the ground is right'. That was another piece of wisdom my teachers had given me.

As it happened, he didn't come again; but this account bears witness to the fact that he was not forgotten. The haunted inn still holds its secret, and I wonder if the malevolent woman has appeared since? Later, when introduced to the work of Rescue Circles, I wondered if it might be possible to exorcise this murderous spirit, but I remember the young man saying that his friend (the landlord) refused to believe in ghosts, although his wife was aware of them. Sometimes red hot coals would be hurled from the fireplace in their living room, and there were other poltergeist activities, but no, the man still refused to acknowledge the phenomena and would certainly not welcome any interference from spiritualists.

Poltergeist activity was also prevalent at the Acre Club which looks on to Windsor's historic (but sadly mutilated) Bachelor's Acre. Hundredweight sacks of potatoes and carrots, stored in the passage way beside the kitchen, were found completely emptied of their contents, the sacks neatly folded on top of the piles of scattered vegetables! This unwelcome feat of psychic strength was repeated several times.

Windsor is, undoubtedly, a very haunted town. The lovely Theatre Royal has two ghosts — unless it is one doing double duty in two parts of the building. A landing at the top of a flight of stairs leading to the offices has a 'chilly feel' to it, but I have not heard of anyone being seen there.

Joan Riley, a director of the theatre, told me something that happened to some young people working as stage staff on one of her productions. Because they had neglected to do certain jobs during the day they were obliged to work on the stage all night to meet the deadline of a dress rehearsal — and shortly after midnight they had seen the ghost of a woman in the balcony. She had 'screamed at them terribly', and they complained of being frightened out of their wits.

'Don't expect any sympathy from me' said the unflapable

Miss Riley. 'If you'd done your work at the proper time, you wouldn't have disturbed her.'

Mary Kerridge, who has probably appeared more often on that stage than any other actress, once told me something interesting about the acoustics. While the theatre was, generally 'good for sound', there was one small spot in the balcony where members of the audience sometimes found difficulty in hearing. I had not heard the ghost story at that time and would be interested to know if this 'deaf spot' was where the young people had seen the apparition.

4

Months passed, with no message concerning Len, but I was resigned to waiting and continued with my prayers. Other people, remembered or forgotten, made their presence known through the mediumship of Elsie or Wilfred. Since some had 'passed over' many years ago, it was necessary for them to delve back into the past for evidence with which to identify themselves. I became even more convinced that mediums do not read our minds.

But there were still many things that remained beyond my grasp. I was totally unable to picture the realms of Spirit. Some books on the subject have been said to be dictated from the other side, or delivered through the form of mediumship known as automatic writing, but I found them, with one exception, unconvincing. *Testimony of Light* was first published in 1969 by the Churches' Fellowship for Psychical and Spiritual Studies, a group of discerning and responsible people who had already been impressed, not only by the author, Helen Greaves, but by another mystic, Frances Banks. Both had helped them in their work.

It was Frances who, after her death, dictated the book telepathically to her mediumistic friend. Its message, quite simply, is that the death of the body is but a gentle passing to a much freer and fuller life. A nun during her time on earth, she found herself rejoining her Community and able to continue their work together. This impressed me since I had already learned of the vast amount that needed to be done for those lost and bewildered souls on the Other Side. Later *Testimony of Light* was taken up by an established publisher, and so gained the wider public it so richly deserved.

Someone who reviewed the book called it 'a glass of Spiritual champagne' and certainly others on the same subject seem flat in comparison. This is not to say they are fraudulent, it is simply that descriptions of the 'higher realms' need a language less prosaic than our own. To speak of pink marble pavements and buildings of beautiful translucent colours conjures up old Hollywood musicals rather than a Heavenly Kingdom.

Another thing I could not accept was the possibility of astral travel. That our spirit left our physical body during our sleep seemed utterly unbelievable, yet there were often references to this in messages as well as addresses. It became another topic to be discussed over the teacups on a Sunday afternoon.

'Haven't you ever had the feeling of falling through the bed, and then being jerked up again?' someone asked.

'Years ago. I was told it happens when your heart misses a beat.'

This caused some amusement. It was, it seemed, the spirit returning to the body, but after a time it became so natural, it wasn't felt at all. I still couldn't believe it.

'Pray to be shown the answer,' said Mrs Crispe, with infinite patience. It must have seemed to her that I'd had so much evidence of the power of Spirit it was high time I accepted things in faith. I prayed as she suggested then promptly forgot about it while investigating some other aspect of Spiritualism. Then came the night of the strange dream-like experience which has remained vividly in my mind ever since.

I was standing alone in a grey, luminous fog, unable to see anything tangible around me. Where was I? What was I doing there? Oddly enough, I felt neither apprehensive or nervous. It occurred to me 'I must be dreaming this', and almost immediately, like an answer, a far stronger thought imposed itself. *This is not a dream.*

There was a bright, shiny key in my hand. Did this mean there was a door for me to open? All I could see was this baffling mist I think it was at this point I was first aware I was not alone after all. While there was no one to be seen, I was conscious of a protective presence, of someone watching over me.

Suddenly, there was movement - the mist, which had been opaque and still, began to gain substance, as if wisps of grey cloud had entered in. It grew darker, colder. There was no sound, and certainly no feeling of a wind blowing, yet these darkening clouds seemed driven by some invisible force. Then, just as suddenly as the movement had begun, it ceased. The swirling clouds seemed to be drawn purposefully downwards, and were falling into shapes, creating a scene before my eyes.

It should not be hard to describe since it was simple, primitive and devoid of colour. It was as if I was confronted by the grey face of a cliff, stretching as far as I could see in both directions. In the face of the cliff were many caves, mostly small and dark, in which I could see crouching figures, one to each cavity. I could see no faces, partly because of the gloominess and also because each figure seemed slumped down in the depths of despair, the face turned away from me.

Why was I able to look at this desperately sad scene with an air of detachment? I felt sorry for these wretched people, yet curiously untouched by their suffering. Perhaps, if I went into one of the caves and spoke to its inhabitant? But when I started to move forward it was as if an invisible barrier prevented my progress. I could not move, only stand and observe. Yes, someone was with me, and while I could not see them, I felt completely under their protection. This must be why I felt no fear. And was it not possible they were also able to control my emotions, so that I was not allowed to be upset?

For there was worse to follow, things were being added to the scene which were truly horrifying. In the gloom between the caves men were hanging on ropes, and there were other poor souls who had also taken their own lives. Once more the thought struck me forcibly - or was it a voice that said, '*This is not a dream*'-? No, I agreed, for if it were it would be a nightmare, and I'd wake up screaming.

As it was I awoke calmly and peacefully and told myself, yet again 'That was not a dream'. Then I lay still, reflecting on what had been shown to me, committing it to memory. It did not seem fitting, at that moment, to make notes.

Instead I obeyed an urge to say my prayers. After that I returned to bed and fell into a natural, dreamless sleep.

With my usual caution, I told no one of the experience. It would be interesting to see if Wilfred or Elsie would be inspired to say anything about it on the following Sunday. There was nothing from Wilfred, but Elsie addressed herself to me in the evening.

'I'm being told you've had your experience of astral travel.'

'Oh?' I said, determined to give nothing away.

'You must know about this,' she insisted. 'I'm told you were taken on a visit to the realms of darkness. This is where you work in your sleep state - you go there because of your sympathy for suicides. Showing you has been a special privilege, but it will never be allowed to happen again.'

There was no further need to be evasive; all I could do was ask one question: 'Why was there a key in my hand?'

She replied without a moment's hesitation. 'The key symbolised the fact that you were about to witness a new psychic experience.'

Afterwards, this explanation was confirmed by other mediums, unknown to each other. One told me the name of the spirit helper who accompanied me on these nocturnal journeys. 'First you are taken somewhere to gather the strength and knowledge for your task, then you administer to those souls in darkness.'

'But why do *I* do this work?' I asked Mrs Crispe. 'There must be thousands of spirits on the other side better able to help them.'

'No,' she told me. 'The realms of darkness are lower than the earth plane, and the density of the atmosphere is such that spirits from the higher realms can only endure it for short periods. Because we are conditioned to the impurities of the earth we can work there longer.'

It made sense, for I remember being told how the higher realms saw the world as a dark, almost impenetrable mass of grey matter, immersed as it were in a slimy coating of mud (created it would seem by the evil thoughts and deeds of the inhabitants). It was not easy for them to pierce this armour even briefly to make contact with us, and if the realms of darkness were worse, it would surely be well-nigh impossible.

'But what do I do when I'm there?'

'Talk to the poor wretched souls. Explain what has happened and assure them that it's possible to escape from the darkness. Then, when they're ready, you pass them on to the spirits who come with a light to take them further on their way.'

So I was able to accept that astral travel is a reality, although the experience was never shown to me again. Later, from a source outside the Sanctuary, I gained further insight into the work done by Spiritualists to help 'those in darkness', and this further evidence is not at odds with the knowledge gained earlier.

It was Ken Taylor, a man I met at the Sanctuary, who told me he belonged to a Rescue Circle presided over by a Mrs Iles, a medium living on the edge of Burnham Beeches. Rescue Circles were a part of the Spiritualist scene I had not been told about, although I was assured that there were many in different parts of the country. Not enough, it seemed, to cope with the demands made upon them. Seeking as always, I asked if it would be possible to join such a circle. Ken Taylor replied that it might be, but naturally the decision rested with the medium.

Mrs Iles was a large lady and I think far older than she hoped to appear. Her hair, dyed jet black, matched her dark eyes, and I doubt if she bothered with her figure. She was cut of a tougher, coarser cloth to dear Constance Crispe - this was no mild, gentle lady - but I liked her and she, I'm glad to say, liked me. She was not intellectual or particularly spiritual, but an excellent medium. Once married to a man who was also psychic, they had run their own church until his passing. As a widow, she had given up the church and concentrated on private sittings and the Rescue work, in which she claimed her husband helped her.

It was decided that I could attend the Circle while another member was away, and Ken Taylor kindly offered to call for me in his car and take me there.

The Circle consisted for two mediums, Mrs Iles and a man called Ron, whose psychic gift she had helped to develop. They sat in armchairs on either side of the fire. There were three other straight-backed chairs to be occupied by Ken, a lady and myself. The room was dimly lit, for subdued lighting appeared to create the right atmosphere for those we hoped to help.

After a prayer, we waited. My new friend on my right appeared to go to sleep, and so did the lady on my left. (They were, I was assured later 'giving out power'). Mrs Iles was carefully watching her protégé, and I wondered if I imagined that his face seemed to be changing?

'Good evening, friend,' said Mrs Iles eventually.

Ron jerked his head, turning in the direction of her voice.

'Who is that -?' It was not Ron's voice as I'd heard it when introduced earlier. He had sounded a bit of a rough diamond, but pleasantly good-natured. This voice was educated but autocratic.

'I welcome you to our Circle.'

The face seemed to be sneering. 'You welcome me, Madam? And where am I, may I ask?'

'In my home.'

'Am I indeed, I did not ask to be brought here.'

'You are welcome, none the less.'

The sneer became even more pronounced, the voice scathing. 'You are very free with your favours - but I am not accustomed to visiting the homes of strange women.'

Mrs Iles looked somewhat amused at the rebuff but was temporarily at a loss. She whispered to me '*You* talk to him - we must hold him as long as we can.'

Not knowing how to deal with the situation I started with a modified form of her greeting. 'Good evening, sir'.

Ron's face was certainly quite different now, as his head turned towards me. 'You know me, sir?'

'No, I've not had the pleasure of meeting you before.'

'I'm seeing a man who looks as if he might have been an army officer.' Mrs Iles whispered. 'He goes way back, and has an ugly wound in his side.'

It transpired he'd met his death, not in battle, but in a duel with another officer. It took a long while to discover this — even longer to convince the proud gentleman that he had finished with the earth plane and should travel on. If there was any truth in what we were saying, where was he to go? No, he didn't believe in another life, or in God.

We spent more than an hour in the presence of this unreasonable entity, but finally he saw the light brought by Mr Iles and his helpers, and they took the reluctant officer on his way.

'You joined us on a difficult evening' said Mrs Iles afterwards. 'We usually deal with two or three people in that time.' Even Ron, who awoke to know nothing of the manner in which he'd been used, felt exhausted. Naturally he wanted to know what had happened, so did the others, equally oblivious. 'I'm no good at history but I'd say he was from Nelson's time' she told us. 'Let's try to get warm — he brought this cold with him — they brought him up from the depths, no doubt of that.'

'The depths' were presumably the realms of darkness. The temperature had certainly fallen during the evening, in spite of the fire. It was explained that a band of workers 'down below' brought people to them as the next step in their progression. Theirs was a half-way house, a rung in the ladder from darkness to light — but our stubborn officer still had a long climb ahead. Eventually, I imagine, he might arrive in the Spirit hospital described by Frances Banks in *Testimony of Light.*

'At least he's on his way,' sighed Mrs Iles. 'There's some satisfaction in that.'

The next Rescue Circle was a far more lively affair, for 'our light' appeared to attract a number of men arriving in quick succession one after another. These were not from the realms of darkness but soldiers recently killed in battle. Confused and bewildered, they had no idea they were dead, and the language that passed Ron's entranced lips would have horrified a lesser woman than the intrepid Mrs Iles. Only once did she look shocked, and it was not through anything she heard. 'I've just seen a man with his head blown off.'

We managed to hold the attention of one man who had, beneath the rough exterior, some understanding of religion. Through him we reached the others, and Mr Iles was able to take five lost souls when he came with his light. There were still a number of soldiers in need of help.

'Can't we work a little longer?' I whispered.

'No, we can't,' said Mrs Iles firmly 'It's after eleven and

Ron can't take any more. You've no idea the demands this work makes on him.'

The soldiers were not there the following week so we hoped some other Circle came to their aid. This time is was another soul from the realms of darkness. Ron appeared to be cringing in his chair while making pathetic whimpering sounds.

'I'm seeing a poor wretched woman in filthy rags,' whispered Mrs Iles, then added her welcoming 'Good evening, friend.'

It would take too long to give a detailed account of this visitor. At first we thought she had been a servant in a big house — but no, 'servant' was too fine a word. 'Drudge?' Perhaps not even that. Almost certainly she was feeble-minded, and possibly crippled, or in some way deformed. All she saw of the house was the great kitchen, and when she was not working (if indeed she did work — for on reflection we did not establish this) she lay in a dark corner of the room. There, on a stone floor, she had lived, slept, and presumably died.

Snatches of her conversation remain with me, together with the pathetic whine of her voice. 'They threw me scraps. They never gave me a bowl. I always hoped they'd give me a bowl.'

It was not easy to raise her above her abject misery, and all the while we endeavoured to 'place her'. Again, she came from 'way back' for such a kitchen, and such treatment, surely belonged to an ugly and unenlightened past. I wondered if she was the imbecile child of one of the servants in the house, allowed to remain under sufferance in those appalling conditions.

Finally, when I could think of no more things to say, I asked again if she ever left the room, and the answer was no. 'Not even on Sunday? You never went to church?' But Sunday and Church were words she'd never heard, and God was unknown to her.

Ken Taylor and I discussed the evening on the journey home. 'There is always one common denominator where the souls from the realms of darkness are concerned. When you speak to them of God, they either don't believe in Him, or haven't been taught of His existence, like the woman tonight.'

'Which is why they are in darkness?'

'Yes. But that woman - it's hard to believe a loving, merciful God would allow her to remain in those conditions just because she'd never been told of Him. It must have been more than a hundred years.'

And there I stopped myself. We were up against time again. For all we knew, a hundred years might be only a minute in eternity. Perhaps the poor soul had not really been long in that wretched state.

I attended about a dozen Rescue Circles in all, and made many interesting discoveries which bore out the teachings of some of the learned souls who spoke through Elsie. One Sunday we were given a long, sobering address on the care of the physical body. It was perhaps no more than an expansion of the views expressed in the Bible, but emphasized that the body was the temple of the holy spirit and should, therefore, be treated with respect and reverence. 'There are many in darkness who bitterly regret having used their bodies for immoral and unnatural purposes.'

As if to prove the truth of that statement we had a Rescue Circle evening visited by prostitutes of both sexes, and certainly a sorrier, more despairing group of lost souls could hardly be imagined. They seemed to have spent a long while in the grim, cold darkness, locked together in a sterile, stifling relationship from which there seemed no escape. Wallowing in sexual activities which brought no satisfaction, they complained bitterly of the plight they were in. While eternal progress is available to each human soul, we could not reach them that evening and went home feeling dirty and depressed. It took a long while to shake off that ugly experience.

The worthy Mrs Iles died some years ago so that 'light in the darkness' was extinguished. I know of no other Rescue Circles, though hopefully they do exist. That there is a need for them, I have no doubt at all. Unhappily they demand the services of a strong sensitive and a number of people willing to devote themselves to a cause which *can* be rewarding, but also contains an element of risk and a number of depressing disappointments.

5

It was on October the 15th, 1962, exactly four months after his passing, that I received the first detailed message concerning Len. It was delivered by Elsie through the kind offices of that same monk who had once said my prayers were helping him. Len was suffering remorse and deeply regretted what he had done, especially the distress and trouble he had caused. He had been in the room when I found him, and had not realized how much it would upset me. (This sounded odd until I remembered his state of mind). My prayers had helped greatly, and he was well on the path of redemption, but prayers were still needed. I gave my assurance they'd be continued. This entry, copied from my note book into my diary, was, after that first exciting communication from my mother, the message I was most grateful to receive.

It was around this time some newcomers started visiting the Sanctuary. What was more, they appreciated the services and managed to persuade Mrs Crispe and Elsie to start a Development Class. While I only had a vague idea of what this involved, I pleaded to be allowed to join. I don't think the ladies were convinced of my suitability, but they were too kind to refuse.

The class was to be held on Thursday evenings in a downstairs room. Six straight-backed chairs were arranged in a wide circle, and the only illumination was a red bulb in a standard lamp and the glow from the gas fire. The newcomers consisted of a married couple, Frank and Enid, and a friend called Jessie. Jessie was also married, but her husband was not a Spiritualist. After the opening prayer, we all settled down to meditate. It looked as if the entire evening was to be spent in this manner.

In the early days I found meditation difficult. I simply could not lose myself, so opened my eyes and watched the others. Once you were used to the dim light, it was possible to see the faces quite clearly, and they were certainly interesting. After a while I realized that every person present appeared to be transfiguring, with the exception of Mrs Crispe, who was as watchful as myself. Most interesting of all was Jessie - she looked extremely unhappy. In fact I could have sworn there were tears on her cheeks.

Because I felt our teacher was eyeing me with disapproval, I closed my eyes and attempted to meditate again, but it was useless. All I was aware of was a faint persistent hissing sound from the old gas fire. Then, some fifteen minutes later, I was aware that something was happening to my face. It felt as if I'd walked into cobwebs. When I attempted to brush the irritant away with my hand, my skin felt curiously moist. Even though I was sitting near the fire, I was not so warm as to be perspiring.

At the end of a long evening, we were asked to say what we'd experienced. Frank confessed to feeling transported back to ancient Egypt, while his wife had been much aware of a guide she referred to as 'her nun'. Poor Jessie, who still looked tearful, said she just felt very, very sad.

'And you, Gyles?'

'I'm sorry,' I said, nothing if not honest. 'I couldn't meditate, I was just aware of the sound from the fire.'

'Is that all?'

'Well, yes. Apart from a feeling of cobwebs on my face.'

'You were being transfigured.' Mrs Crispe sounded almost cross. 'Your Chinese guide. I saw him distinctly, but you brushed him aside.'

But it wasn't my failure to co-operate that disturbed her. She was concerned about Jessie, and rightly so, for when we arrived for the lesson the following week a serious conversation was taking place.

'She's been depressed all the week, suicidal, in fact -' Enid was saying. 'I doubt if her husband will allow her to come tonight.'

'I sincerely hope he does,' said Mrs Crispe. 'It's clear

she's possessed, and we must do something about it.'

'We're sorry we introduced her.' Frank apologised. 'It seems she's too gentle and sensitive for this sort of thing.'

'It's really nothing to be alarmed about,' explained Elsie. 'Just one of those unfortunate things that can happen to someone with her sympathetic nature. She's attracted the spirit of a woman who recently committed suicide - so many of these poor souls come to us, attracted by our light. If she comes this evening, Constance and I will deal with the situation.'

Jessie arrived. The change in her during one week was appalling. She looked as if she'd had no sleep, and dissolved into tears the minute she entered the hall.

'She's not herself at all,' whispered Enid. No, she was not. She didn't even look like the calm, neat woman we had met the week before. No wonder her husband was concerned about her.

During the evening, while she sat gently weeping, I saw Mrs Crispe and Elsie leave their chairs and go to her side. They held out their arms, moving them upwards, as if she wore some long garment that reached to the floor, and they were raising it up, up - until their arms were fully extended upward. It looked as if they finally tied an imaginary bow above Jessie's head.

I was witnessing an exorcism, and whatever ritual those remarkable women performed in those few silent minutes, I can only say it worked. The sad mask was lifted from Jessie's face, and she opened her eyes, sighed deeply and whispered, 'She's gone.'

Mrs Crispe said it had been a wonderful experience. She and Elsie had seen the spirit of the wretched suicide 'rise up and leave the body.' Jessie was given instructions on how to protect herself, but it seemed to me that possession was something that could happen all too easily. And what had become of the soul of that poor woman? She had left Jessie, and we were all greatly relieved - but where had she gone?

The Development Class had not started well. Jessie was not allowed to attend again, and I was the next to fall by the wayside.

'You have been transfigured by several guides. You know what that means? They'd like to use you for trance mediumship, but you put up barriers. You won't let them come through.'

'I'm sorry.' It had to be said. 'I don't want to be a trance medium.' It seemed almost blasphemous to say so.

'But my dear boy -' (regardless of age, we were all boys and girls to Mrs Crispe) these are *wise* men - beautiful souls - if only you'd dedicate yourself to the task, take it more seriously, you could give trance addresses, like Elsie.'

'I'm sorry,' I said stubbornly, 'Elsie hasn't a clue what's been said through her until tapes are played back afterwards. She doesn't even know who it is. I wouldn't like that. It's too great a responsibility. I want to *know* what I'm talking about.'

While sadly disappointed, I think she could see the sense of my argument. I was not a 'pure vessel' and unlikely to become one, so perhaps it was inadvisable for me to be used in trance. The guides, who certainly do exist, commented kindly on my decision, through Elsie. They quite understood the brother's unwillingness to be used in that manner - but they would still be around to help and inspire. If I sent out thoughts and questions, they'd endeavour to answer them for me.

One thing was certain, there was work for me to do, and they wished to help me do it.

☆ ☆ ☆

While my interest in Spiritualism had brought me new friends, some of the old ones 'gave up on me' about this time, and I couldn't blame them. They acknowledged the help I'd received at the Sanctuary, but hoped I'd eventually become as I was before Len's breakdown. But I was never to be that person again. Some said I'd lost my sense of humour, and it was something I wondered myself.

'You take everything so seriously,' they would say.

'But life is a serious business.' I'd tell them, full of my new found knowledge, and would start on a long tirade which must have made me as tiresome as the most persistent Jehovah's Witness.

I lost all interest in theatre and cinema, and activities at the Sanctuary took precedence over all else. It was a long while before I began writing again, and when I did my work had curious esoteric overtones which made it unacceptable for the popular market.

'I only hope there's a sense of humour on the other side,' said a resentful friend after I'd persuaded him to attend a service at the Sanctuary. The address had been particularly long and dour.

True, humour seldom, if ever, broke through there, but I have a little story which seems to suggest that a sense of humour does exist among the spirit friends.

It was a few months after moving in to the Garden Flat that the incident occurred. It was my habit to wake about eight, and this gave me ample time to do the necessary jobs and be down at the book shop around nine-thirty. I awoke this particular morning with a tune in my head, a silly old music hall song which I could not identify. Music hall had been dead for a long while, and I had not heard anything of the kind for years.

The tune persisted while I leisurely bathed and shaved and I became increasingly irritated that I could neither forget it or recall its name. Vaguely, by reaching deep into my memory, I began to associate the song with a female male impersonator, but even her name escaped me.

Someone was ringing the doorbell. It was the daily women who'd forgotten her key and hoped one of the tenants would let her in. She looked surprised, and slightly abashed on seeing me, for we worked on a system of trust, and she was, in fact, late.

'What time is it, then?' I asked, assuming it to be about half past eight. It was almost eleven. I'd overslept at least two hours.

It was only when I was hurrying through the town that the music hall song identified itself. It was almost as if a woman was singing it in my head: '*I'm Burlington Bertie, I rise at ten-thirty-*' It must have been ten thirty when I rose from my bed! It was now after mid-day and while my employer was not unduly concerned with time keeping, I certainly expected the shop to be open. Instead, there was a phone call to say he was ill. It did not altogether surprise me, for while he had not complained he had not looked well for a considerable time. Unhappily, the illness was more serious than anyone imagined, and the kind, gentle man died a few months later. The shop was closed, and my useful little job came to an end.

Since the writing remained singularly unfruitful I would have to find something else, but I wasn't worried. It was as if, through the Sanctuary, I had learned not to worry. You took your troubles to God and left them there. To continue to feel apprehensive was to doubt His ability to help, and having been helped before, I had no doubts. While reflecting on this, I almost collided with Canon Fisher of St George's Chapel.

'I'm sorry to see the book shop closed down,' he said kindly. 'Have you anything else lined up for yourself?'

'Not yet,' I replied.

'You wouldn't care to come back to the Chapel? Just while you're looking?'

I hesitated. It looked, on the face of it, a step backwards.

'You could be a big help to us,' he went on. 'We're starting a new scheme selling tickets from an office outside. We need someone reliable to check them when they're given up.' To further arouse my interest he added, 'I think we can do a little better in the way of salary.'

So I returned to St George's Chapel. After all, I argued, I had nothing to lose, and had made a few friends there. It was like old times, the familiar surroundings, and members of the staff breaking the monotony of the day by telling me their troubles. The sacristans, Ray and Bob, were feeling a little sorry for themselves. Cyril Grimmer, the third sacristan, a man older than themselves, had been ill for several weeks, and while they were not unsympathetic, they were tired of performing his duties as well as their own.

I remembered Cyril. He and his wife Doris lived, like most of the Chapel staff, in the Horseshoe Cloisters nearby, and Doris, bright and efficient, had undertaken to join the ticket office staff. It was a little job she could do while still keeping an eye on her sick husband, and during slack moments we talked about his health.

'He doesn't seem to get any better,' she told me.

'What exactly *is* the trouble?'

'His doctor says it's rheumatoid arthritis. He's prescribed pills and a liniment to rub in. The pain seems mostly in his back and I give it a good rub every night, but it doesn't seem to help.'

I wondered if Spiritual healing would be beneficial but was too cautious to broach the subject. I did suggest I might give her a break by taking on the task that evening. The offer was accepted. Cyril seemed pleased to see me, and I spent some fifteen minutes rubbing his back. While I knew little of healing, I silently prayed that this 'laying on of hands' was helping in some way.

It was my evening for the Rescue Circle, so I hurried back to the flat, fed Simon, washed and changed, and literally ran for a bus which would take me within walking distance of Burnham Beeches. For some reason Ken Taylor was unable to call for me that evening, and I arrived some minutes late. The group were sitting in silence as I slipped guiltily into my chair.

After a few minutes, Mrs Iles opened her eyes and looked at me. I thought I was going to be reprimanded, but was fortunately mistaken.

'Before we start I must speak to you Gyles. Your Father is here, and he's been explaining why you are late. He tells me he was with you when you visited the sick man earlier this evening, and he says, very lovingly, *you should not have rubbed him.* It is not the right treatment, for his illness has been wrongly diagnosed. I feel you will be hearing more of this.'

Next morning I could not avoid a very worried Doris as I entered the Chapel. Cyril, she said, had had a dreadful night, quite the worst he'd suffered so far. 'I'm going to get a second opinion,' she said. 'I feel sure his illness is wrongly diagnosed.'

It was. Poor Cyril had cancer of the spine, and died a few weeks later.

6

During the weeks that followed the position of Sacristan at St George's Chapel was advertised in the *Church Times*, and we heard from the office, there were many applicants. Men started arriving for interviews, some with excellent references from similar posts, so why were the Dean and Canons so long in reaching a decision?

The delay was hard on Ray and Bob, for it was now months since they'd had time off. Their wives, too, were complaining bitterly. One morning, when Bob was airing his views on the predicament, I made what I thought to be a little joke. 'I think perhaps the Dean and Canons are waiting for *me* to apply.' To my surprise, instead of smiling, he took me seriously. 'Have you thought about it?' he asked.

'Good heavens, no! I was only joking,' I told him. 'I couldn't do what you and Ray do - talking to the public, serving at the altar, and that sort of thing.'

'I don't see why you shouldn't fit in,' he said. 'Why don't you think about it? The salary isn't bad, especially for a single man - and you'd have somewhere to live.'

'I've got somewhere to live,' I pointed out, wishing I'd never made the feeble joke.

After he'd left, I tried to dismiss the matter. True, I had my rent-free flat and had lived there happily enough for more than two years. But all was not well with the flatlet house. Repairs were needed on the roof and a law had recently been passed that all such buildings should have a fire escape. Cissie was not facing up to these necessities. While reaping a good income from the property, she was most reluctant to spend money on it.

A home in the grounds of Windsor Castle would be interesting, and the salary more than acceptable, but then I tried to see myself as a sacristan and thought it quite ridiculous. And yet, when I met the verger's wife on the way home, I found myself saying: 'I had quite a joke with Bob this morning -', and repeated what I had said earlier. Her reaction was identical to his, and again I denied my suitability, wondering why on earth I'd started the nonsense a second time.

I'd hardly been home more than a few minutes when the phone rang. It was the verger's wife to say she'd spoken to her husband. He thought, as she did, that I had the makings of a sacristan and would be willing to train me. He'd just gone to the Chapel for Evensong, but would have a chat with me tomorrow.

I hung up the phone in a state of sheer panic, appalled to think where my foolish chat had led me. I had only myself to blame. What could I have been thinking of, to say what I did to Bob - and then, regretting and rejecting it - repeating it again to one of the few people who were in a position to carry the preposterous idea a step further?

But there was one big stumbling block which might, for good or ill, put a stop to it. The advertisement read, '*Third sacristan wanted for St George's Chapel. Must be communicant of the Church of England.*' And I had not been confirmed. But when the verger talked to me next day he said that this, while regrettable, need not stand in the way, for there were Confirmation classes starting in the near future.

Things were happening too fast and I begged for time to think them over.

'Better not take too long,' he warned. 'This is a *very* sought after position remember. There are plenty of applicants - some highly recommended. But I'm the Dean's right hand man - he *listens* to me - and he'll not make a decision without consulting me first.'

This was not strictly true, for the gentleman had an exaggerated idea of his importance, but I was not to know that then, neither did I care. I only wondered why I was so favoured.

'St George's is a Royal Peculiar,' he went on by way of

explanation. 'We do things *differently* - so it's no use people coming here with preconceived ideas. I must say, I rather *like* the idea of training my own man.' There was the clue.

Never before had I been in such an agony of indecision. On one hand, it looked like an opportunity, but I still could not see myself within that framework of orthodox religion. While the world of entertainment was no longer important, it was still the only sphere I knew. Suppose I got the job and was found to be unsuitable? I'd have burned my bridges and lost my flat. On the other hand — there was Cissie allowing the house to fall to pieces. A year or two more would be the most I could look forward to.

Before going to bed I prayed for the answer, but it didn't prevent me having a sleepless night. Then I spent my free day seeking advice from my friends. They listened long and patiently, only to say, 'It's up to you, isn't it? No one can advise you. It's a decision you must make for yourself.'

'What about your friends at the Sanctuary?' someone suggested. 'You might get a message about it.'

I had thought of Elsie. She did not give sittings, but might be inspired to tell me something. But I'd learned already that, having made friends with mediums, it was inadvisable to seek their advice. Because they know your circumstances, and are in sympathy, their natural concern for your welfare 'gets in the way' of their clairvoyance. They are aware of this themselves. So Elsie would not do, and neither would Mrs Iles. Then I remembered hearing of 'a good little medium in Slough'. Her name, when I finally traced it, was Margaret Downs, and I phoned for an appointment.

The call, from a phone box, was brief and to the point. Yes, she could see me the following afternoon at three. I was about to give my name when she said 'No, I don't want it. I'd sooner know nothing about you. Come at three.'

That was all. So when I called next day she not only didn't know my name but had no idea where I came from.

It was a neat, brisk little brunette who opened the door and showed me into her front room. 'I'd like you to sit in that armchair and simply say yes or no to anything I give you. And please don't mind if I walk about all the time. I can't seem to work sitting still.'

'May I take notes?' I asked.

'Yes, but I work rather fast. You might have trouble keeping up with me.' She closed the door and the sitting started.

'My guide was with me when I opened the door,' she said. 'He told me 'This is a man in a state of indecision -' (so much for my carefully rehearsed nonchalance). 'Yes or no?'

'Yes.'

'There's a twofold reason for this. The decision involves not only where you would work, but where you would live?'

'Yes.'

'They're showing me a picture. I don't know where it is - could be town or country. But it's on high ground, with one or two trees. The important part is an old, half-timbered house. There's scaffolding around it — men at work. Great care is being taken to maintain the old look. Can you recognise what I'm describing to you?'

'Yes.' I was quite convinced it was Marbeck House. Built in the outer walls of the Castle it was the home of the organist and the place where the choir boys practised. It was being restored, and not only that, a flat was being made in the basement.

'If you were to make this decision, would you live in this house?'

That stumped me for an answer, for while the flat was being made for *someone*, it might be anyone on the Chapel staff.

'Well, yes - it's possible, I suppose.'

'And would the place where you'd work be only a few yards away?'

'Yes.'

'That's what I want.' The lady, who seemed to be enjoying herself, continued her pacing. 'I've got your father here. He says it's thanks to him you've come here today. I think he's had a lot to do with the whole business. He says he twice popped the idea into your head. You understand that?'

'Yes.'

'But now he's standing aside for another gentleman. This man is taller, very military, he -' she suddenly burst out laughing. 'Oh dear! He's just said, "Don't waste time, woman - tell him it's his Uncle George!" '

This was exactly the way my Uncle George would behave, but he was the last person I expected. When I was a boy he was strict and severe, and I was half afraid of him. My sisters sought to assure me that he mellowed in his old age, but I chose to keep my distance.

'Your Uncle is saying he knows this place well.' And since he'd been head choir boy in the time of Queen Victoria, there was no denying that. 'He's come to say there's no reason at all why you shouldn't do this job. I don't know what it is - he's not telling me - but you *can* do it, and he thinks you should.'

If Uncle had spoken to me like that when I was young, I would have automatically gone against his advice, but I recognised now his wish to help, to compensate for the harshness he'd shown me as a child. 'They try to put things right,' Mrs Crispe had once told me. 'It's sometimes very difficult to find the opportunity, but they can't make progress unless they do.'

'I've a lady here now. She says when you first knew her, she was blonde. Then, when you met after the war, she was a red-head. She says, "What silly vanity it all was, for she was never blonde or auburn" '

This extraordinary description delighted me, for I recognized immediately a wonderful woman friend who had never communicated before.

'This lady wants to remind you of a conversation you had in Bristol, not long before the blitz. You were standing at the open window on the top floor of a tall building, looking out at the view. Do you remember this?'

'Yes.' I recalled it exactly. We had enjoyed looking at the old roof tops, and counted the church spires. Irene had said: 'I think it's important to have a nice view from a window. If you can't, you must have a beautiful picture.'

'She is saying that if you do as they hope you will, you'll be living somewhere with fine views. That's what she's come to contribute this afternoon.'

'Oh, please-' I said excitedly, 'I know I'm only supposed to say yes and no, but I must thank her and say I know she's Irene Lines.'

'She was fading as you spoke, but she turned and gave you a little wave, more like a salute.'

It had been a gesture I'd seen her use frequently in her lifetime.

The amazing sitting continued for fully an hour. One by one they came through, family and friends all giving their carefully considered reasons why they wanted me to apply for the post of sacristan. It was marvellously organised, clearly they had come together to make this concerted effort on my behalf. It was as if each had been given just so many minutes in which to make their point. Then towards the end - 'I have a young man here. I feel he's not been over long, and I sense a tragedy, but he doesn't want to dwell on that. He hasn't learned to communicate but just wishes to associate himself with what the others are doing.'

Len.

'I hope it's helped you,' said Margaret Downs.

I told her it had been a fantastic experience, and yes, it had certainly helped. 'I know now I must apply for this job, but I doubt if I'll get it.'

She smiled confidently. *'You'll get it.* With all those wonderful people behind you, you couldn't do anything else. You know, this has been a marvellous experience for me too. Don't think I find all sittings as easy.'

As she opened the door she paused and said, 'I really shouldn't ask this because it's none of my business - but has this anything to do with Royalty?'

'I suppose you could say that. Why?'

'I've just seen the Royal Standard flying from a flagpole on a Round Tower. This wouldn't be Windsor Castle?'

Because she deserved the satisfaction, I told her it was.

Leaving her house, I felt like walking on air. A truly evidential sitting has this effect, and apart from that, I felt there was such a weight off my mind. I must have walked nearly a mile, pausing to peer at my notes, reliving every revealing minute. Was Margaret Downs an exceptionally good medium? With due respect, I would now doubt this, although she was certainly gifted. In retrospect, I believe that sitting, so splendidly organized on the other side, would have reached me equally well through Elsie or Mrs Iles, had I gone to them. When we are facing a crisis the loved ones in Spirit are determined to help; all they ask is a channel through which to communicate, and anyone with a psychic gift would have been used for the purpose.

Reading my notes for the third time in fifteen minutes, I was suddenly struck by a remarkable omission. Of all the people who'd gathered to prove they had my interest at heart, there was one notable absentee - my mother. Father, uncle and my eldest sister had put in an appearance, but not the one member of the family who had hitherto come first.

I stopped to take stock of where I was, for this residential quarter of Slough was unknown to me. Then I thought, since I wasn't far from Burnham Beeches, I might call on Mrs Iles. I'd heard she was ill, so bought a bunch of flowers. 'I must be careful not to mention the sitting,' I told myself. 'She might be hurt to know I've been to someone else.'

She was sitting up in bed, looking far from well, but brightened up considerably at this unexpected visit.

'You know you haven't come alone, dear,' she said as I sat down. 'You have your mother with you.'

7

An an act of faith, I wrote my letter of application that same evening and dropped it in the letter box of the Chapter Office. Four days later the telephone rang. It was Canon Hawkins, Steward of St George's Chapel, an elderly gentleman approaching retirement. A tireless worker, he was constantly in and out of the building, but always found time for a friendly word, or at least, a gentle smile.

'I understand you are due at the Chapel at eleven, Mr Adams?'

'That is correct, sir.'

'Well, I wonder if you could make it a little earlier today? Shall we say half-past ten? Would you be able to do that?'

Greatly wondering, I replied that I would.

'And when you arrive, would you call on the Clerk of Works, Mr Pratt? He will show you the basement flat of Marbeck House. Perhaps I should say the basement that is being *made* into a flat. I fear you will find it in a deplorable state, but I do assure you, our workmen will make a splendid job of it. We'll leave it like that, then. I'll tell Mr Pratt to expect you.'

I hung up the phone in utter bewilderment. Clearly this had something to do with my letter, but not a word had been said about it. Then the phone rang again. 'Oh, Mr Adams, I quite forgot to tell you - when you've seen the flat, will you call at the Chapter Office?'

The basement of Marbeck House had not been used for years and was certainly deplorable. At some time in its long, long history the rooms had been kitchen quarters. There was a big open space where an oven had been, and beside it a dumb waiter to carry meals to the floor above; but it must have been many years since it served this purpose. There was a line of damp three feet from the floor, and the plaster had fallen from the ceilings. Jet black cobwebs hung from the rafters and cupboards, riddled with woodworm, had been ripped out and lay about the floor.

But the room in which we stood was a good size, long, with windows at either end. One opened only onto a basement area, but the other, some hundred feet from ground level, commanded splendid views. Over the roof of the Theatre Royal I could see the Thames, and beyond this, the fields of Eton. *'If you do what we hope you'll do, you'll be living somewhere with lovely views -'*

The Clerk of Works was eyeing me anxiously.

'Canon Hawkins has asked me to make sure to tell you how nice it will be,' he said. 'But it puts me in quite a spot. If you're not happy, I'll be the one you'll be chasing all the time.'

'That problem might not arise,' I told him. 'I haven't been interviewed yet. But tell me - was this flat being made for the new sacristan?'

'Not necessarily. If he'd been a married man, he'd be offered a house. The Steward thought, since you're a bachelor, a flat would be more suitable.' So the decision had not been made before the Dean and Canons received my application! It was all so incredible, I longed to tell this nice man (or, for that matter, anyone who'd listen) the extraordinary predictions made a few days earlier. As it was, it was time for the next appointment.

The oak-panelled Chapter Office was nothing if not impressive. Light streamed down in patches of rich colour from the high, stained-glass windows, and the Canons of St George's, seated around a long oak table, might have been sitting for a painting by Rembrandt. The Dean had recently departed for Cyprus, but even without his august presence it was a daunting scene. There was only one lady present, the Chapter Clerk, mouse-like in grey.

Canon Hawkins opened proceedings by asking if I'd seen the basement, and what did I think of it -?His concern was quite touching.

'It's charming,' I said. 'I could move in tomorrow.'

This irresponsible reply seemed to cause some amusement. Even stern Canon Bentley, at the head of the table, showed the flicker of a smile.

The architect's plans were unrolled on the table. Had Mr Pratt explained? That would be my living room, and next was the kitchen, then the bathroom, and finally my bedroom. That dotted line was where a wall was to be built across the passage.

'Oh, no!' I said to my own surprise. (Who was 'popping things into my head' this time?).

'Dr Campbell wants to keep the two end rooms.' The Chapter Clerk spoke in a tone that suggested she didn't altogether approve of me.

'Whatever for?' asked Canon Fisher. 'He's the whole house upstairs.'

'Utility rooms. He needs somewhere to wash and dry his clothes.'

'But I must have a second bedroom,' I insisted. 'I might want someone to visit me.'

'Of course, that's perfectly reasonable. He should have the larger of the two rooms - the one at the end of the passage.' This from Canon Fisher. 'Dr Campbell's staircase can go down to the smaller one.'

Still nothing had been said about the job itself. What we were having was a lively discussion over the accommodation, the central heating, and other necessities. And from that we went on to the subject of Simon. Pets were not encouraged, but I wasn't coming without him.

It was Canon Bentley who cleared his throat and brought the meeting to order. 'I see from your letter, Mr Adams, that you've not been confirmed?'

This remark had a sobering effect upon the assembly, the plans disappeared from the table, and faces assumed serious expressions.

'No,' I admitted. 'I was to have been, but my family moved from one place to another and somehow it never took place.'

'You would be prepared to be confirmed if we made the arrangements?'

'Oh, yes.'

'Very well, then. I think it only remains to offer you the

position of Third Sacristan, and hope you'll be happy here.'

They rose, and each shook hands while wishing me well. I thought them charming and kindly gentlemen, and nothing was ever to happen to change that opinion.

Where the job was concerned, it was a question of being 'thrown in at the deep end.' Someone found me a sacristan's gown and I began to patrol the Chapel, to keep an eye on things and hopefully answer questions. Ray and Bob were quick to catch up on their time off, and I didn't see much of the verger either. Sooner or later it would be part of my duties to give talks to parties of tourists. I asked if there was any 'set piece' and was told it was up to me to make up my own, so in quiet moments I studied the guide book and tried to memorize the more important dates.

One afternoon I heard a commotion from the direction of the Canon's Cloisters. It was the Dean, a big, exuberant gentleman who seemed incapable of going anywhere without a great deal of noise. 'On duty now, is he?' I heard him say, 'I'll go and see.' He entered, approached me with a big, beaming smile and clasped me in a warm embrace. 'My dear fellow, it's good to have you with us!' he assured me. 'Your letter came the day before I left for Cyprus, and I said to my Canons, 'You needn't look further as far as I'm concerned - that's the man for me!'

His kindness was the more surprising since we had done little more than pass the time of day during my duties as doorkeeper. 'I've told my Vicar to come and see you about your Confirmation,' he said before leaving. 'You know the Bishop of Reading has consented to take the service? It will be here, at the High Altar.'

The Dean's Vicar was one of the busiest men around the Chapel. He was as active as the Steward and it seemed curious that so much of the administration fell upon the shoulders of the oldest and youngest members of the resident clergy. I had never spoken to the young man and was sorry to think I was to add to his burdens.

By the time he called on me at the Garden Flat I had worked myself up into something of a state. My first few weeks as sacristan had been especially tiring, for I was not only on my feet all day, but also had the journey to and from the Chapel to contend with. None of this mattered as much as the new problem which now confronted me. It was all very well relatives and friends in Spirit urging me to apply for the job - now that I'd got it I had something of a conscience over the matter. While I had never been anything else but a member of the Church of England, it was Christian Spiritualism which had brought me to a fuller understanding of religion.

While I didn't consider myself a Spiritualist, I felt deeply indebted to the Sanctuary of St John the Divine. There were bound to be conflicting loyalties. Should I contemplate Confirmation feeling as I did? The Dean's Vicar, a man young enough to be my son, played the unexpected role of Father Confessor that evening and was never to open the books he had brought to help with my preparation. I told him everything hitherto related, and after he'd listened patiently for hours, awaited his verdict.

Since we were strangers until that evening, it wouldn't have surprised me if he'd doubted the things I'd told him, but I don't think he did. 'I think you've been very fortunate, arriving at your religious convictions in that manner,' he said. 'I'm sure many members of the clergy would have been glad to be brought into the ministry through such an experience.' And he didn't see any stumbling block to my Confirmation. I was deeply grateful for the help he gave me that evening.

On the evening of Wednesday, 22 June 1966, I was confirmed, by the Archbishop of Reading, at the High Altar of St George's Chapel. The Dean, the Very Reverend Robin Woods, his vicar, Reverend Ian Collins, and a few others were present. The simple ceremony was nicely stage-managed by my colleagues, Ray and Bob, and there was music by the assistant organist, Peter Williams.

It was rather overwhelming. What was I *doing* in this scene of historical splendour, where men were made Knights of the Garter, and Royal Christenings, weddings and funerals had taken place? Somewhere beneath my trembling knees was the vault containing Charles I, Henry VIII, and his Queen, Jane Seymour. I had been told, at the Sanctuary, that many of my loved ones would be present. I wonder if they were as mindful as I, of the honour bestowed on me that day?

During the months that followed my psychic notebook remained unopened and even my diary had only the briefest entries. 'Led Choir into Evensong', 'Confirmation', 'Serve at the altar for the first time'. And sometimes brief notes recording the progress the flat was making. 'Area steps made today'. Mr Pratt and his men were unsparing in their efforts to make my new home comfortable, and any suggestions were carried out without murmur. Meanwhile, I found a man to take over the flatlet house so Cissie need not feel let down by my departure.

It was early summer when Simon and I moved into Marbeck House. My cat's behaviour on arrival almost gave me a heart attack. He had *not* liked being carried down the basement steps, thinking perhaps, we were to live in a cellar, and on being put down in the living room he'd rushed across the room and leapt up on the windowsill, as if seeking escape. Luckily I managed to grasp his magnificent tail while he looked down and realized the danger he was in, so high above the pavements of Castle Hill.

One of the places I could see from that window was the roof top and grounds of the Choir School, at the foot of the hundred steps. It was here I was taken by Ian Collins to see something he felt would interest me. On the walls of a corridor were large framed photographs showing groups of earlier choir boys, and one, dated 1888, showed George Miller as head boy. He looked very proud and pleased with himself.

'I also made another discovery,' said Ian. 'The boys did not become boarders in this school until a few years later. There were dormitories in Marbeck House.' *So my uncle had actually slept in the house which had become my home almost eighty years later!* I had told my friend many strange things, but even he thought this a rather uncanny coincidence.

A little more than a week later something happened that had me reaching for my notebook again. I'd returned to the flat and sat down for a rest before starting the evening meal, and it was probably some time before I noticed the dull, metal object on the seat beside me. It was a thin, misshapen cross, four inches long and two and a half inches wide. It was decidedly unusual, roughly made, almost sharp on the edges, as if made by someone without proper tools.

It was certainly not a manufactured article, and looked a bit rusty, dirty even, as if it had been buried somewhere.

Nobody had yet come to visit me in my new home and even if they had called while I was out they would hardly leave such an unusual object on my settee. And I felt quite sure it had not been there when I left for Evensong, hardly an hour before. I had heard of apports - articles transported by Spirit agencies from one place to another - and could only suppose I now held one in my hand. But where had it come from? I thought of the Curfew Tower, barely a hundred yards away. There, at some time in history, foreign soldiers had been imprisoned in the dungeons. Was it possible this cross had been made by one of them, and had lain for many years buried there?

It was an intriguing thought, but I warned myself not to be too fanciful. There was another question, the answer to which might be less interesting but more important. Where it had come from might remain a mystery - but why had it been brought to me?

'The house in which you live was once the home of a great man,' Elsie was to tell me later. 'He was deeply religious and devoted the greater part of his life to the Lord's work - indeed there was a time when he almost died for it. The saying of prayers in that house was a way of life in those days, and he's interested that you have gone to live there. He left behind a great deal of Spiritual power which could be used for prayer.'

Was the man John Marbeck, the 'Father of English Church Music' whose lovely work is heard to this day? It seemed natural to think of him, since the house bore his name, so I went to the library and discovered what little I could. He had been born around 1510 and died about 1585, but there was doubt about both dates. A married man with two sons, he was organist at St George's and produced a plainchant setting of the Book of Common Prayer (1550). His great work was a Concordance of the Bible. He certainly sounded a deeply religious man.

It was further stated that he had been tried and condemned for heresy in 1544, and his Concordance confiscated. A term of imprisonment followed, but he had finally been pardoned by Henry VIII on the plea of

Gardiner, one of his chief accusers. Remembering the times in which he lived it seems highly probable that he almost died for the courage of his convictions.

☆ ☆ ☆

In the evening, when the last of the tourists have been ushered from the grounds, the Castle and its precincts become a quiet and private place. After Evensong, the clergy and choirmen retire to their quarters in the Canons' and Horseshoe Cloisters, the boys to the Choir School at the foot of the hundred steps. The military knights are snug within the grace and favour houses in the Lower Ward, and, if the Queen is in residence, the Royal Standard flies from the Round Tower, and lights can be seen in the wing of the castle occupied by the Royal household. But there are few people about, especially in winter, apart from the police at the Henry VIII gateway and the guardsmen on duty within the grounds. It is only at such a time that one can sense the history and imagine how it might have been to live there long ago.

It was Samuel Pepys who acclaimed Windsor's castle 'the most romantic in the world', and few would quarrel with that description. While we know that William the Conqueror selected the hill as a site for a fortress, it is difficult to establish an exact date when the building of the castle commenced, though it is mentioned in the Doomsday Book of 1084. But while undoubtedly very old and romantic, it is not as rich in ghostlore as one might imagine. Of all the monarchs who resided there, only two are reported to have returned to haunt it — Elizabeth I and George III.

Elizabeth was psychic and had a vision of herself on her deathbed shortly before her passing. Within days her spirit was seen walking in the Queen's Library, and later on the North Terrace, the making of which had been her personal contribution to the castle. It was her favourite walk. George III, sadly insane towards the end of his life, was confined to the Round Tower and said to be seen, after his death, looking out the window. I never saw either of these Royal spectres during frequent walks in the grounds and suspect their haunting had ended long since.

Perhaps the most famous ghost was that of Herne the Hunter, a warden of Windsor Great Park in the time of Henry III. This formidable individual was suspected of witchcraft and hanged himself from the branch of a great oak which afterwards bore his name. Herne's Oak was struck by lightning in 1863, but for long after his ghost was said to prowl the park, usually seen where the great oak stood. Old prints depict him with antlers on his head, like some wild huntsman of Norse mythology. It was said that whenever he appeared, cattle fell dead and trees withered.

One unhappy spirit recorded in the history of hauntings, is, I suspect, still around, though one wishes this was not so. Some fifty years ago a young guardsman shot himself while on sentry duty in the Long Walk. Weeks later, another guardsman, an eighteen-year-old grenadier, was patrolling the spot in the early hours of the morning when he saw a figure marching towards him. He thought at first it was his early relief, but the face beneath the man's bearskin headdress was that of the comrade who had shot himself.

I know the guardsmen at the Castle were unhappy about that guard duty and only recently there was a newspaper story that a young soldier had fainted on seeing a ghost. The report was played down and the officer in charge suggested the man was over-imaginative, but I have my suspicions. I also wonder why, in this enlightened age, it is not possible to acknowledge the existence of spirit people.

That there were hauntings in parts of the castle there was no doubt, and the Queen was said to have expressed an interest in the psychic phenomena which took place. This curiosity might well be inherited. It is now common knowledge that Queen Victoria was deeply involved in Spiritualism, though keeping this a secret in her lifetime resulted in a good deal of unworthy speculation regarding her association with a member of her household, John Brown.

Brown, who had been the Prince Consort's personal servant, was a natural psychic, and after the death of the beloved Prince Albert the 'widow of Windsor' spent most of her evenings behind locked doors, making contact with her husband and keeping careful note of the communications.

It is not difficult to imagine the gossip whispered among the Queen's ladies, for Brown, a dour Scot, took full advantage of his unique position and ruled the Royal household with a rod of iron. Little wonder they smarted under his authority. How could the Queen allow such a rude, rough man to behave as he did, and why was his company so important to her?

King George V (our present Queen's grandfather) is said to have found great interest in Victoria's 'psychic diaries' and they might cause a sensation if published today, but it is perhaps right that her hard-earned secret should remain a private affair. One or two mild plays have been written about the Queen and her Highland Servant, but the far more interesting truth of their relationship was not made known.

8

'Now concerning Spiritual gifts, brethren, I would not have you ignorant,' said St Paul to the Corinthians, and it seemed without my seeking, many of these gifts were being shown to me. The discerning of Spirits, speaking in tongues, prophecy, healing. As for the working of miracles — it all came under the heading as far as I was concerned.

There were also lesser gifts practised by Spiritualists, and one of these was psychometry. The word is derived from the Greek words psyche, meaning 'the soul' and *metron,* signifying 'a measure'. So by this definition, psychometry is the power to measure and interpret 'the soul of things'.

My introduction to this was on a first visit to the headquarters of the Spiritualist Association of Great Britain at Belgrave Square. This large house, visited by people from all over the world, is a hive of activity. There are lectures and demonstrations of clairvoyance in two large halls, a chapel and an entire floor devoted to healing. Also a bookshop, restaurant and a number of small rooms used for groups and private sittings.

I joined a group of six people and waited for Mr Harold Sharp. He was, they said, a veteran medium, one of the best, but I hadn't attended a group before and didn't know what to expect.

'It's psychometry,' said a lady, and she slipped a ring from her finger and placed it on the small table. A gentleman contributed a bunch of keys, and finally there were six items there, all a little separated from each other. 'They shouldn't touch,' the lady continued and looked at me for my contribution. I was wearing a watch which had belonged to Len - but I'd replaced the worn strap with a chrome expanding bracelet. The two together looked equally new.

Mr Sharp entered, sat down, and looked at the items before him. He then picked up my watch, closed his eyes for less than a minute, and said 'I get two distinctly different vibrations on this. I feel the watch is older and conveys feelings of suffering and tragedy. I think it belonged to a very sensitive person who took his own life. A gentle, kindly soul. The bracelet has a much livelier feel to it. I think this belongs to a man who is very reserved, not shy, but reserved.'

I give no more than that, sufficient to say the charming old medium was extremely accurate, not only regarding Len but also myself. Shy I have never been, but always reserved, especially at this moment of time in a room full of strangers.

Mr Sharp asked who the watch belonged to, and as I claimed it, enquired if I understood the reading. Then, as he handed it back to me, he said, 'You live somewhere where there's a great deal of Spiritual power. Could you start a Circle there? It would be greatly blessed. This isn't psychometry, by the way - just something I felt I must say to you.'

The majority of mediums are women and it may be said that while a few are excellent, there are many less gifted and some who should not be practising at all. Male sensitives are few. I met only three at Belgrave Square, but they were all, in their individual ways, remarkable. I have already written of the late Harold Sharp and his gift for psychometry. Another gentleman, who was visiting as a guest medium, was William Redmond, and my sitting with him was certainly memorable.

After giving me convincing evidence of survival, he surprised me by asking 'Do you believe in reincarnation?' I replied that it was something I'd not made up my mind about.

'If you have an open mind on the subject I will tell you something of your previous lives,' he said. 'You've been on the earth plane many times before and my guide is telling me you had a particularly good life in North Africa. If you ever go to that country you will find yourself happy and at home there. It's as if you left money in the bank. You'll like the climate and the people - especially the Arabs.'

I smiled and told him, 'I think I've had that experience,' for I'd lived in North Africa for two years during the war, and seemed to be the only soldier who was happy there. I had indeed felt as if I knew the country, and was aware of a particular warmth and sympathy for the Arab population. Much as I wanted to return home when the war ended, it saddened me deeply to leave Algiers.

When I told Mr Redmond this, he said, 'Well, now perhaps you are able to accept reincarnation as a fact. Tell me, how do you feel about small cell-like rooms?'

A curious question to which I had no reply.

'I ask because I saw you in such a place. I'm being told you were a monk in your last life. You lived in a monastery near Brussels. Only a few walls remain now, and the fields in which you gathered herbs have been built over. You were very frustrated then because it was an enclosed order, and you weren't able to meet people and speak to them on spiritual subjects, but *now* you have chosen not to wear a monk's habit or a clerical collar. You mix freely with men and women of all denominations or of no religious convictions whatever.'

Since visits to London were infrequent, it was usual to make the most of them. Once, a West End show would have completed my day, but I had lost all interest in the theatre, and much preferred to return home around seven, on a quieter, less crowded train. I liked to read over the copious notes made during the sittings, and often things that had not made sense would fall into place.

Redmond's evidence of reincarnation had impressed me because it accounted so plausibly for my love for North Africa. And now, as I thought about it, the reference to a small, cell-like room stirred something in my memory. When you have lived a long, full life, it is hardly surprising that memories of childhood fade, but they were now coming back.

My home had been a large, five-storey house, and at the top, on a half-way landing, was a big, empty cupboard, built into a recess about ten feet square. If it had had a window, it could have served as a tiny room. As it was, it was my secret place, somewhere to hide when visitors called. But it had been more than that, and I felt a growing excitement as the memory came flooding back.

It should first be explained that I was far from being a religious child, and hated the weekly visits to the local church. The service, an hour in length, seemed endless to a small boy who understood not a word of it. I would sit beside mother, squirming with resentment, promising myself that when I was old enough to please myself I'd never go to church again.

And yet I could not have been more than seven when I modelled a cross out of clay, and when it had hardened, painted it. For I remembered now that I had taken it to my secret place and hung it, with difficulty, on one bare wall. And there I would go from time to time, and kneel before it. I do not recall if I actually prayed, but it was odd behaviour for a boy who was in no way religious.

And what was my hide-out but a small, cell-like room?

There was another strange thing connected with that time. My favourite, solitary game was played with small, wooden bricks. I'd arrange them in rows, and each brick represented a boy or girl in a classroom. I was their teacher, yet I did not like my infant school and was certainly unaware of any wish to become a schoolmaster.

Some people say the pattern of children's behaviour may indicate the path they should take in life, but it can also signify a road they may have travelled in the past. I had to wait forty years for the explanation to those mysteries.

Having been introduced to psychometry, it occurred to me that the rusty metal cross, which appeared so mysteriously in my flat, might have a story to tell. Mr Sharp was not available, but the receptionist at Belgrave Square was most helpful. 'If it's psychometry you're after, why not go to Kathleen St George?' and I was fortunate enough to get an appointment with that popular medium.

Mrs St George held the cross in both hands, closed her eyes, and remained silent for several minutes. Then she told me: 'This was made by a man out of his desperate need. It took a long while to make, but time was of no consequence. I feel he was imprisoned somewhere. He hadn't the tools for shaping it, and his hands bled over the task, but that didn't matter either. He wasn't a native of this country - French perhaps? Certainly a devout Catholic. He treasured this cross - many fervent prayers were said over it.'

So my guess regarding its origin was not short of the mark, and I could accept that it had been made by a prisoner of war in the dungeons under the Curfew Tower. I could well believe his hands bled, for the edges beneath the grime and rust were sharp and rough. How he fashioned it at all was miraculous!

After the reading Mrs St George was interested to know where it was found, and I told her of the curious circumstances. 'An apport,' she said, as if they were in no way unusual. 'You should accept it as a blessing on the work you are to do. I think this must be a holy place. Have you any idea of its history? I think the cross was brought to you for a special reason — it marks the spot where something should happen. Would it be possible to start a Circle there?'

She was confirming what Elsie had said about Marbeck House, and both ladies had suggested that a Circle would prosper under that ancient roof. Well, I wasn't unwilling, but was it quite the thing to do, in the shadow of St George's Chapel? How would I go about it, and who would join me?

The first person I thought of was Ken Taylor and it was probably because he was mainly interested in healing that I decided to go ahead. A Prayer Circle mainly devoted to Spiritual Healing could hardly be objected to.

The next person approached was a lady *in need* of healing. Wendy Harbord had recently taken on a new appointment as Accountant. Concerned with salaries, insurance cards and other matters, it was not an easy job, and there were times when she was literally at the end of her tether. As the season progressed and the Chapel filled with tourists, I also needed healing. Because I was the last to join the staff, evening opening sessions were added to my normal day.

The Circle started, in a very small way, on Friday, 11 October, 1968, and it was soon apparent that our healing prayers were being answered. There were many grateful letters bearing witness to this, and more names added to the healing list. It was inevitable that our Friday night activity became known in the Community and while we did not draw attention to what we were doing, it never occurred to us to make a secret of it.

The police at the Henry VIII gateway were certainly aware since the few members of the Circle living outside the Castle had to be admitted after the gates were closed. I don't know who originally said that London's policemen are wonderful, but the men chosen for duties at the Castle are among the best. John was one of the younger men on the force, friendly like the rest, but with a natural curiosity regarding our activities. When I heard that he had for some years suffered with severe migraines, I suggested he should come to us for healing, and the evening of his first visit will not be forgotten by those present at the time.

After the opening prayers and absent healing, a stool was placed in the middle of the floor and John sat on it for Ken's administrations. We worked in silence in those days (later we played quiet music) and while the contact healing was taking place the rest of us meditated. I was naturally interested in watching Ken at work.

When the session was over, the young policeman seemed reluctant to leave the stool but sat with a bemused expression. 'May I say something?' he whispered. 'Something strange happened the moment Ken put his hands on me. I felt a click in my head and then saw myself up in the corner of the room, looking down.'

We could only agree that it was a strange, psychic experience. It was not until later we learned of the pineal gland, located in the head slightly behind the pituitary. Science has not discovered the function, if any, of this gland; many psychics believe it may be the doorway through which the astral body is released, and have observed feeling a *distinct click* in this part of the head when embarking on an out of the body experience.

John left the stool and sat on one of the chairs to join us in meditation but the young man had further surprises in store for us. As he sat with closed eyes, dwelling no doubt on the strange happening, I noticed the suspicion of a sheen on his face, and suspected the presence of ectoplasm.

This is the strange substance I'd felt on my own face and knew could transfigure our natural features, placing, as it were, a mask upon the face. And surely enough, he began to change, his pleasant young features becoming quite different - the nose flattened, cheeks wider - there was even a thickening of the lips and a straightening, as well as a darkening, of the hair.

Wendy, who had never seen a transfiguration before, gazed in amazement, but it was not frightening. The new face, negroid and alien, still managed to radiate good will and kindness towards us. It remained for some minutes before melting gently away. John looked himself again, opened his eyes and smiled. The owner of the face had introduced himself to him in that brief time. He judged him to be an Aborigine, his name was Mogu and he indicated he was his friend.

So the policeman who came to us for healing was a natural psychic, and his migraine (which he admitted had been so bad as to make him suicidal) ceased from that first visit. Was this through healing? Partly, perhaps, but since he was clearly full of psychic energy we could not help wondering if it was that that caused the headaches. Once in an atmosphere where the power and tension could be released, his physical self functioned normally.

It was too much to expect that a young man, discovering an unsuspected and interesting side to his nature, should keep the matter to himself, and this I could appreciate, since I'd wanted to share my own experiences. It wasn't long before he was practising psychometry (for which he had a natural aptitude) in the Police Lodge, and while some of his colleagues were impressed, others made fun of it. While we were unaware at first, none of this reflected very well on the serious work of our Circle.

But policemen, while they may not admit it, are more psychically intuitive than most. The reason given is that during their early training, while out 'on the beat', they train themselves to watch, listen, and register impressions. This is what happens in a Development Class, the difference being that the lonely policeman walks the streets at night instead of sitting in a darkened room. Psychic gifts, as observed earlier, are not the prerogative of religious people, although this is not to say policemen are not religious.

The police at Windsor Castle became my friends and some of them confided in me about impressions they picked up in parts of the Castle which are undoubtedly haunted. One man was checking the State Apartments when he passed a woman in a passage way. It crossed his mind that he had not recognised her as one of the household staff, turned to take another look, and noticed she wore a dress that trailed the floor. Then, as she turned a corner, she 'just faded away'. Would anyone else have seen her? Not necessarily. I think he had reached that degree of awareness.

At the time of the bomb scare a new alarm system was installed at the Castle. If someone were to walk through a beam of light, it would sound a warning in the Police Lodge and Guardroom. There were many false alarms and men installing the system said there were often 'teething troubles' in old places, and admitted to the considered possibility that ghosts could be responsible.

'Is that possible?' asked one of the more sceptical policemen. 'Would ghosts have the strength to set off burglar alarms?' They certainly could. It's a good job they haven't a mischievous poltergeist around, or they might have alarms every night.

☆ ☆ ☆

This would be a good place to say something about Sensitives, or Mediums, as they are most usually known. People who have never met any often have mistaken ideas of these much-maligned men and women, misled, no doubt, by the way they have been depicted in books, films and plays. Perhaps I've been specially fortunate during my years of seeking, for while some are more gifted than others, I've not met one who hasn't been kind, helpful and sympathetic in his or her work, and humorous, well-adjusted and thoroughly down-to-earth in personal life.

High on my list came Muriel Miller and Kathleen St George, and while they are elderly ladies both are young in spirit and age is something you do not associate with them.

In truth, they were born about the same year, but it might be said they represent the old and new schools of mediumship. Kathleen is a 'mental' medium, while Muriel belongs to the vanishing race of transfiguring sensitives. I have seen her transformed into an elderly Indian, a young French nun, a vital Spanish lady, a coloured child and a number of other people, all within the space of an hour. She allows her own spirit to stand aside while possessed by another, but this is acknowledged to be a dangerous practice, should she encounter some form of shock while allowing herself to be used in this manner.

There is nothing weird or spooky about my sensitive friends and it would be a mistake to imagine that every meeting with them is a 'sitting' or out-of-this-world experience. 'When I'm not working I close myself right down,' said Muriel, and it is certainly very necessary they should do so. But sometimes, in their company, an odd flash of inspiration creeps into an ordinary conversation.

During the first week of December I remember Muriel saying: 'Are you likely to be presented to the Royal Family this Christmas?'

'Good heavens, no!' I told her. 'Whatever put that idea in your head?' But she just smiled knowingly, and would not be drawn on the subject.

Sacristans do not get 'presented' but play a very humble part in the scheme of things. I recall a ceremony in the Chapel when the Queen gave me a long look as if to say 'I haven't seen that one before'. A few words with the Duke when he asked me if I'd seen someone, a friendly good afternoon from the Queen Mother, and always a lovely, warm smile from Princess Margaret. That was the full extent of my encounters with the Royal Family and I didn't expect it to extend further.

Then came a midnight service on Christmas Eve, to be attended by all the 'Royals' with the exception of the Queen. My colleagues were all doing the honours in the Quire while I stood in the Ambulatory awaiting the arrival of Prince Charles. It had already struck the hour and the Dean, to my horror, turned to me and said: 'I must start the service - *you* must show his Royal Highness to his seat.'

It was the last thing in the world I wanted to do, involving as it did some ceremony (which I hated) bowing to the Altar when entering and leaving the Quire, and doubtless a certain amount of bowing in other directions also. All this before a glittering assembly and under the critical eye of the verger who, while never honouring his promise to train me, was always quick to draw attention to the fact that I hadn't learned the 'niceties' of the job.

I went outside the door and hoped fervently the Prince would not come, but footsteps could be heard coming down the hill and the young man appeared accompanied by his detective. I should have known how to deal with the situation but I didn't. No formal bow, no ceremony or properly chosen words. I grabbed the Prince by the arm and said 'Buck up, you're late!' How we appeared on entering the crowded Quire heaven knows, but we managed it somehow, and when I returned to the Ambulatory the detective had a grin on his face.

'Hardly the way to behave to our future King,' I told him.

'He'll not care about that,' he said cheerfully.

It could be said, perhaps, that I was 'presented to Royalty' that Christmas, though hardly in the approved manner. Perhaps that was why Muriel had smiled and said no more.

The incident had an amusing sequel a few days later, when the Prince came into the Chapel with the Dean, to see something of theological interest. He recognised me, smiled and asked 'Have you forgiven me for being late, yet?' I liked Prince Charles. He is a warm, sincere man with a good sense of humour. Much has happened to him since these brief encounters. He has married, become a father, and shown an interest in psychic phenomena. Did he have this interest at that time? Had I thought so I might have told him of our Circle.

If you work for the Royal Family you are asked to sign an agreement that you will not disclose anything of a private nature learned while in their service. Fair enough, but some unscrupulous people have broken their promise and written all manner of nonsense for financial gain. As a member of the Chapel staff, I wasn't asked to sign anything, so I'm free to say I found them all quite splendid, both on and off duty, and more than worthy of both our love and respect.

9

If Wendy had not been working late in her office she would not have received the phone call. It was intended for the Dean and Canons, but the numbers were listed together under the heading of St George's Chapel, and the caller, in his state of agitation, dialled her number in error.

Believing as I do that there is a reason for *all* our actions, I can only suppose the message was intended to reach me in this round-about manner, yet there were those who said we should not have responded to the call. Perhaps it was to help three frightened people, for the man who sought the clergy so urgently was desperately in need. The flat in which he and his wife lived was haunted and they'd suffered one terrifying experience after another.

Wendy did not know how to go about contacting the Dean and Canons at that time in the evening, and also doubted whether they would wish to be involved in the matter. I suppose it was only natural she should think of the Circle and give the worried man my phone number. He was almost hysterical. The flat, in Windsor, was at the top of an otherwise empty house, and they'd had trouble ever since they moved in. His wife was under sedation and he didn't think he could stand much more. Wasn't there such a thing as exorcism?

There was, of course. Whether anyone as inexperienced as myself should have tackled it is another matter. Fools, they say, rush in where angels wouldn't, and I was all for rushing in. After all, there was the Rescue Circle experience behind me - it was probably simply a question of talking to the earth bound spirit and persuading it to go.

But I'd need the help of a medium and thought immediately of John. He was definitely psychic, and the fact that he still had much to learn never occurred to me. I phoned his home in Eton and he agreed to come at once.

So we started off for the haunted house, two misguided innocents eager to accept the challenge. John keen to test his new-found skills, and me, feeling as always the surety that we would both be protected, and no harm could possibly come to us. We decided, on the journey, the way in which we would handle things; John didn't want to be told anything but wanted to sense things for himself.

The house, standing on its own grounds in one of the quiet, residential roads was tall and Victorian. Only the top windows were lighted while those below looked very dark indeed. We knocked and lights appeared on the staircase and in the hall. A young man hurried down the stairs and opened the door to us. He was, we later discovered, a hair stylist and the girl he introduced as his wife was probably in the same business. They wore matching slacks and sweaters, and both looked equally scared.

The bare hall and uncarpeted staircase had been painted red, an angry colour which should be used sparingly. It did nothing to warm the place for it seemed colder inside than out. We explained that we wanted to be told as little as possible, and asked if we could go over the rest of the house. There was no reason why we shouldn't, for all but the top floor was unoccupied, the rest still being converted into flats.

Left to ourselves, John and I examined each room in turn, starting in the basement and working slowly upwards. Unfortunately, the electricity was not connected, so all this investigation was carried out in the dark. John would stand for a few minutes sensing the atmosphere, then say 'Nothing here', before we moved on. Eventually we reached the top floor where the young people awaited us, accompanied by a girl who was staying with them. She too, looked frightened.

'I only seem to sense something in the hall and on the staircase,' John told them.

They were in agreement. At night, after they'd locked the front door and returned to the top flat, they would hear the door thrown open and then slam shut, to be followed by footsteps on the stairs.

I suggested we should sit in the hall and see if we could contact the cause of the trouble. John, I explained, was a transfiguring medium, so they mustn't be surprised if his appearance changed. I also told them of Mogu, who we now accepted as John's guide, and who I fervently hoped would be there for his protection, and indeed ours as well.

We each took a chair down to the cold, gloomy hall and made a circle of five. I sat on John's right and next to me was the girl-friend, then the man and the woman. I led them in the saying of the Lord's Prayer and then, to my great relief, saw Mogu transfigure John and greeted him as a trusted friend.

'You know why we're here, Mogu. There's something wrong in this house - someone who shouldn't be around. See if you can find out and tell John about it.'

Mogu had not yet learned to speak through John. Whether this was because of a language difficulty or an inability to master the use of his vocal chords, I do not know. He certainly had no trouble in mentally expressing himself to his medium, and even an onlooker was able to gather a great deal from the expressions on his ugly, good-natured face.

He faded, John's face returned to normal, and after a few seconds he opened his eyes. 'There's a sad woman here who lived in this house long ago. She had a child who was severely handicapped, but she loved him dearly. It seems he completely disappeared while she was away one day, and she's been looking for him ever since.'

The young people looked surprised. It was clearly not what they expected. I asked John if he could bring her through, so that we might talk. 'I can try', he said, and closed his eyes again. It seemed we waited a long time in that cold hall, but it was probably only a question of minutes before we perceived a softening of the features, and a sad woman's face. Unhappily, she could not speak either, but the tears flowed freely.

I used the Rescue Circle technique and explained that it was no use looking for her child in this house. There were those who would help her find the boy, and she would discover he had journeyed to a happier place. 'Look for a light,' I said hopefully. 'People will come with a light - follow them and they'll help you.'

The sad face faded and Mogu reappeared again. He seemed happy, and when I asked if the talk had helped, he nodded. I asked if there was anyone else there, and he indicated there was not, so I said a closing prayer and told the young people there was not more we could do.

The events of the evening had impressed them, but they were not satisfied. It was no sad lady who'd been scaring them, but a most unpleasant man. 'I can only say he's not here now,' said John.

We were invited upstairs for coffee and I asked if I might see the flat. It consisted of living room, double bedroom, kitchen and bathroom, all very bright and modern, but we did not stay long. John had told his wife he'd only be away an hour or two, and we'd been there longer than we thought.

However the young people might feel, we felt we'd done a good night's work. We discussed it on the journey home and voiced our opinions of the people and the flat.

'Did you notice there was only one bedroom?' asked John.

'Yes,' I replied, in all innocence. 'And a king-size bed.'

'No guest room,' observed John. 'I was wondering how the girl-friend managed, that's all.'

'Perhaps she sleeps in the living room,' I said charitably, little knowing how that brief conversation held the key to the haunting.

We had certainly not solved the young people's problem. Early next morning the man was on the phone again. 'We've had a worse night than ever!' he asserted, as if it was our fault. 'An hour after you left we heard the door open, the footsteps on the stairs. Later on I was thrown across the bedroom.'

'Did you see anyone -?'

'No, but Penny did, and she's terrified. She's taking my wife's sedatives. We can't go on like this, living on tranquillizers. What are you going to do about it?'

Since I didn't like the man, or his attitude, it crossed my mind to tell him to find someone else. Instead I told him the decision did not rest with me, but I'd contact John.

In my heart, I knew I wanted to see the matter through, and so would my friend. But it was not easy for him, a married man. His wife was already unhappy about this new development in his life, and now he was to explain that it might be necessary to be away all night, for clearly the haunting reached its peak between eleven o'clock and midnight.

'If you can't come I'll have to see what I can do on my own,' I told him, but luckily he was able to be there and the five of us were seated in the hall shortly after eleven.

Again the Lord's Prayer and once more the comforting appearance of Mogu, but as he faded from John's face we were aware of the ghastly chill that seemed to creep up from the floor. I had lost all feeling in my feet and legs and felt absolutely nothing would give me the power to get up from that hard, uncomfortable chair.

John sat with the front door a few feet behind him. It was locked, bolted and chained. The hall light, high above us, was a feeble, unshaded bulb, and the dark red walls disappeared into shadows.

'I've been told something about the history of this house,' said John, after a long silence. 'Years ago it was a brothel, and the man who troubles you was a frequent visitor.'

And suddenly it was clear to me. The man was drawn back to the house because of what was happening. I recalled the story of the young man who had attracted the woman with murderous intent to the room in the hotel. *Like attracts like.*

John was silent again. I closed my eyes and wondered if it was possible to die of this intense cold. If only something would happen - anything would be better than slowly freezing to death. And then, phenomena began with the sounds of footsteps on the gravel outside, the noise of the front door flung open and slamming shut again. But when I opened my eyes the door was still locked, the only differences showed in John's face, slowly changing before our startled eyes. Whoever had entered the hall had entered him also, and was taking him over.

I was used to seeing John transfigure but never to

anything as revolting as the face we saw now. One eye was completely smoothed away, to be replaced with a scarred lump of unhealthy looking flesh. His mouth twisted up at one corner while the other seemed drawn down almost to the chin. No make-up artist, working for hours, could have created an effect more horrible, and no actor project more evil.

The girl grabbed my arm and whispered: 'That's the face! The face we see at night!'

Meanwhile, the one jaundiced eye looked at each one of them in turn. A lecherous, appraising look for the girls and one of sheer loathing and hatred for the young man. In my enlightened state I understood the thought of this discarnate mind. The call had reached him in the darkness (for surely he was from the darkened realms?) the brothel he'd visited was open again, and he'd come to seek his pleasure. Doubtless he wondered why this man should have two women when he had none.

It was up to me to say something and I took what I hoped was a strong line. 'So it's you who comes here frightening these young people?'

The pock-marked face turned slowly towards me and it was my turn to feel the scrutiny of that evil and expressive eye.

'Don't you realise all this is behind you now? You've finished with the earth plane -'. But the look of sheer contempt and disbelief was too much for me.

Eventually the face faded and it was a great relief to see John looking himself again. 'I'm sorry,' he said. 'But he told me he has a perfect right to be here and has no intention of leaving.'

'See if you can get Mogu back,' I asked in desperation. 'He may be able to suggest something.'

Mogu obligingly reappeared and I asked if there was anyone who could help. To my joy he smiled and nodded, then became John again.

'When you asked Mogu if there was anyone who could help, he suggested your mother, Gyles, and then I saw she was here.'

This shouldn't have surprised me, for I might have guessed mother would come on this mission, if only for my own protection.

'Your mother says this is a very difficult situation. They can't *make* the man go until he's willing to do so. But she promises that while they try to persuade him, the young people will come to no harm.'

We went home exhausted.

Next morning the young man called on me personally and I didn't have to ask what sort of night they'd had. 'God knows what you've started!' he said angrily. 'There were lights appearing everywhere and the whole house stinks of incense. I think they've been burning it in every room.'

'Interesting,' I said. 'They must consider it helps in some way.'

'But we want it to stop!' he was in a foul temper. 'Do you know what happened? We had a *nun* standing by the bed all night! My wife and I don't want that!'

I have a temper too. 'How dare you come here and talk like this!' I told him. 'My friend and I spent two nights trying to help you because you were scared out of your wits, and you have the audacity to complain! And don't talk to me of your wife when you know she isn't! If you hadn't been misbehaving yourselves you wouldn't have attracted the beastly man in the first place!'

The remark regarding the 'wife' was an inspired guess, but he did not bother to deny it in his haste to leave. I learned later, through the police, that she was someone else's wife — not that it mattered, for I was never to see either of them again.

The girl-friend called the same evening and told me something of herself. She was, she claimed, an actress, and there was a part waiting for her in a North of England pantomime, if she could get there. That was, of course, the reason for her visit, so I gave her the fare. She did write later to say she was the Fairy Godmother in 'Cinderella', and 'just loved playing to the little kids'. She wasn't much more than a kid herself, and that was the last I heard of her.

Shortly afterwards I received a spirit message concerning the sad woman who had haunted the house in search of her boy. She was happy and grateful because she had found him, so something good was to come of that adventure.

Months later the telephone rang in the middle of the night and I found myself listening to a wildly hysterical woman. It proved eventually to be the hairdresser's lady. It seemed they were having a blazing row and she feared he might 'do her a mischief'. Bangs and crashes could be heard in the background. Could I go and talk to him?

'Are you still in the flat?' I asked, playing for time.

'No, no — we left there — we're in a bungalow in Henley.'

That decided me. There was no way I could go there at that time of night, even if I wanted to (which I certainly didn't!).

'Let me speak to him,' I suggested reluctantly.

He was even more hysterical, but eventually calmed down sufficiently to tell me a garbled version of their quarrel. He was blaming her while she screamed denials in the background. 'Go to bed and don't say another word to each other,' I told him, and repeated the advice to her also '*Not one more word*', and I hung up the phone on their whimpering.

So they had left Windsor, and I wondered why? Had the horrible man appeared again, or was it the protective nun at the bedside who had driven them away? The trouble was that such people were their own worst enemies, carrying with them the seeds of their destruction. Like would continue to attract like, and if the evil, lecherous spirit had not followed them from the flat there were, unhappily, plenty more where he came from.

That people can become the prey of evil spirits, there is no doubt. Mrs Crispe once told me: 'Most of the crimes committed are planned, set in motion, by earth bound spirits who were criminals themselves.' Knowing, from experience, that ideas can be 'popped into your head', I do not doubt this. A weak intellect, inclined towards dishonesty, could be easily influenced, just as Jessie, in the Development Class, had been persuaded towards suicide. The implications are frightening, and while one longs to deter violence I could not advocate a return to capital punishment, since the murderer might well have been possessed when committing the crime.

This is not to say he bears no responsibility, for he must

have opened the door to allow evil to enter. The young people in the flat had literally invited the unpleasant spirit and he had 'turned nasty' when made unwelcome. If he had chosen to take possession of the young man and urged him to commit murder during one of his rages, you would have such a situation.

10

The scene was the church in Adelaide Square towards the end of a service and the medium was giving clairvoyance, but these were messages with a difference.

'I can hardly believe what I'm seeing with the lady at the end of the second row,' he began. 'You have a bird on your shoulder, a cat on your lap and - yes, there's a dog as well!'

The lady was delighted. 'Yes, I can accept all three! They got on well together. The bird was -'.

'Don't tell me!' said the medium, who then proceeded to describe each pet in detail and give its correct name. 'Now I want to go to the back, the man in the corner, you've a horse looking over your shoulder.'

'When I was a boy -' began the man.

'It doesn't matter when it was, he's here now.'

The medium, whose name I unfortunately do not remember, obviously was a man with a great love for animals, and was therefore used to prove that some of them survive 'death'. No people were mentioned in this clairvoyance, only 'the dumb friends' or what Spiritualists call 'the lesser creation'.

Am I suggesting then, that animals have souls? Yes, to the degree in which we create a loving, spiritual understanding between them and us. This survives their physical death and continues all the while we remember them with affection. If they are forgotten they join the 'group soul of animals' consisting of millions of poor birds and beasts which are slaughtered daily, and never know the affection necessary for their spirit to become a soul, and so enable them to break away from that inevitable fate.

Spiritualists believe we are one with nature and therefore have a responsibility towards all creation, not only animals and birds, but flowers, plants and trees. They have, I think, a heightened awareness of the beauty in nature, which is in itself a joy, but unfortunately you cannot have this sensitivity without suffering more than most when you hear of cruelty and vandalism.

But to return to animals, what should be our attitude towards them, and to what degree should they be loved? Not *more* than mankind. Instinctively one feels mankind should come first, although there are many who feel an animal more faithful, loyal and loving and so *deserving* of the greater part of their affection. How often do we see the 'lesser creation' behaving better than the greater, and how wrong people are who say 'they live like animals' when animals do, in fact, live and behave better than the humans they are endeavouring to describe in a derogatory manner.

Mine was an animal-loving family and a few hours after my birth the family cat jumped up on mother's bed with a tiny black kitten in her mouth. You might say the cat family lost no time in worming their way into my affections, for the kitten became my first pet and lived to a great age. Black cats are considered lucky in this country (the reverse in America). Have I been lucky? In health, certainly, and probably many other ways. But cats have always been important, especially Simon, since he was around at this important time.

I have already written of the way he helped me as a kitten, but by the time we moved to Marbeck House he was a full grown cat weighing more than sixteen pounds. In the evening we'd go for walks in the grounds, often visiting the kitchen entrance to the Castle where the police had an office and would entertain us. Simon would sit at my feet looking from one to another and then follow me home again, but we always had a little trouble when reaching the dark section between Chapel and Deanery.

Simon did *not* like the Canons' Cloisters, before we reached it I could see him growing tense and sensed his fear of entering. Yet he would not let me pick him up and carry him. It was something he had to face alone and it was fascinating to see him literally screwing up his courage, the ears flattening and his half-Persian coat fluffing up to make himself look ever larger. Then he would suddenly plunge like a jet-propelled rocket into the darkness.

When I emerged a minute later the other side of the Cloisters I'd find him waiting anxiously to see if I had made the journey safely, and then all was well. (Later, one of the police told me he had an uneasy feeling of being followed when passing through the Canons' Cloisters at night or in the early hours of the morning. I cannot say I ever noticed anything, but again may not have reached that degree of awareness.)

When Simon was ten years of age he became ill with a bladder complaint and I took him to the vet, where he remained several days. The trouble was serious, and a minor operation had to be performed daily to relieve the pressure of water which could not be passed naturally. He had never been away from me before because, if I couldn't take him on holiday, I didn't go. The vet must have tired of my frequent enquiries and said he'd let me know when there was any change in his condition. I felt he was avoiding me.

It was my day off from the Chapel and I was too miserable to do anything but mope about the flat. Hopefully, to take my mind off things, I turned out the lower shelves of a cupboard filled mostly with old newspapers and magazines. Someone had given me a pile of back copies of the *Psychic News*, and I'd hardly found time to glance at them. Was it by chance, then, that I gave myself this task to do, and found a copy with the front page headline: 'Healer saves famous horse?'

The news item concerned a man by the name of Tom Hoben who believed himself in touch with St Francis of Assisi and had cured innumerable birds and animals. He lived at Kingston-on-Thames, but he wasn't in the phone book so I decided to go and see him personally. He wasn't at home when I called at his humble little house, but his sympathetic wife said he'd be back from work soon. The living-room table was cluttered with a mass of correspondence; requests for healing and letters of gratitude. Mrs Hoben said she was sure her husband wouldn't mind me reading them. There was one from a farmer grateful for the recovery of a cow, and a letter from a little girl giving thanks for her guinea-pig.

Tom Hoben arrived, a middle-aged, delicate looking man who looked as if he knew suffering. (After a long fight with illness, he was to die of cancer a few years later.) I cannot recall the features of his face, only the kindness and gentleness it radiated while I told him of Simon.

'Have you got a photo of him?' he asked.

I had a snapshot Len had taken.

'And where is he now?'

I gave him the address of the vet. 'You're not going there?'

He smiled. 'No. *I* won't be going - but I'll go up to my Sanctuary now and pray for him right away. You go home, and don't worry, he's going to be all right.'

I went home and telephoned the vet around six o'clock. He and his partner had left for the day and I spoke to the young woman in charge.

'Mr Bowditch said he'd phone me and I haven't heard,' I told her. 'I know my cat has to be operated on every day, and isn't eating. I can't let him go on suffering.'

'Which cat is he?'

'A big tabby.'

'I've just seen him,' she said. 'He had a good supper of minced chicken.'

'You can't be talking about my cat, he's not eaten for days.'

'Then he's just been making up for it. He ate *all* his supper and was quite playful. We've only one tabby.'

Mr Bowditch was only too happy to phone next morning. 'I don't know what's happened to your cat, Mr Adams, he seems to have taken a new lease of life. If he goes on like this, you'll have him back before the weekend.' I called for him on the Thursday expecting to find a pathetic creature, but he looked magnificent. His reaction on seeing me was curious. The vet brought him in and placed him on the table beside his basket, but he paid no attention to me at all and rubbed himself against the man's hands, as if thanking him for his services. Strange, I thought, he must have done many unpleasant things to him, yet he seems to realize it was all in an effort to help him. Finally, still paying me no heed, he jumped in the basket to be carried home.

Once there, I expected him to want to take stock of the familiar surroundings on leaving the basket, but no - first of all, I was to get the full treatment - the greeting I'd expected earlier. He climbed straight on to my chest purring loudly, and began the pummelling with his large paws. This was one of his peculiarities. It consisted of a pressure with the right paw, then two with the left and one with the right again, working up to a steady rhythm. He'd be gazing into my face all the while, and the weight on my chest was considerable, but this was the good morning and good night greeting, and the pummelling would continue until he grew tired. He was glad to be home.

But the new lease of life was borrowed time and after a year in which he was never healthier or more affectionate, the same illness overcame him again, and I rushed him to the vet. There was no time to get in touch with Mr Hoben, for while I contemplated a visit to Kingston. Mr Bowditch phoned to say he had died on the operating table. 'Would you like to come and see him?' he asked, but I couldn't face it. During the days that followed I felt guilty about that, and wondered if I should have done.

Then, about two weeks later, while I lay in bed one night, I felt the sudden weight descend on the foot of my bed, and the equally heavy tread of his paws pressing the bedclothes down beside me. It was the feeling I'd known hundreds of times and lay on my back in readiness. I felt the weight of his body on my chest and then the pummelling began; the right paw once, the left twice, the right once more — but with less strength. I heard no purring but said, 'It's my dear old Simon —' and went to put my arms round him, but he was no longer there. He'd just had the strength to manifest sufficiently to show me he'd returned from the vet.

Months later, Len made his presence known through Mrs Iles. He wanted me to know of the work he was doing meeting men who had 'gone over' in the same manner as himself. 'It's not unlike the work you do in the darkened realms,' he explained, 'And the work done here in the Rescue Circles. I belong to a group who take them further on their way.'

Before he left, I asked if Simon was with him. He had

loved that cat and shown him every kindness, but Simon had always been a 'one man cat' and never had time for anyone but me.

'No, you might have guessed, he's chosen to stay with you.'

Kittie Simpson visited the flat shortly afterwards to demonstrate her healing methods to members of the Circle. As she knelt before one of her patients she remarked quite casually: 'You know your cat's here? He keeps brushing against me.'

Other sensitives also assured me he was still around. So this was why, after that one sad day of his death, I didn't miss him. I couldn't understand this, and neither could my friends, for I'd grieved for months over cats that had meant less. But there was the explanation. While I could not see him, my subconscious was aware of his presence.

☆ ☆ ☆

During the ill-fated Development Class I had been told of my spirit helpers and given the assurance that they would come to my assistance in times of need. I was naturally curious about these entities and was advised to have a sitting with Mr Jack Mackay, a sensitive who specialised in describing Guides. There were, he discovered, a number interested in my development, all under the direction of 'a stern and powerful Egyptian'. There was a North American Indian who would help with healing, and an ancient Chinese gentleman who would give me wisdom.

Mr Mackay went to some trouble to explain our delicate relationship with those who have volunteered to accompany us on life's journey, and I was given some idea of what they could, and could not do. We were at all times master of our fate, and while they may lead us to advantage, give us strength in adversity and consolation in times of grief, there were occasions when it would be necessary for them to stand aside while we made important decisions.

Theirs was a humble and often difficult role, and in order to understand it we must first ask ourselves *why* they have chosen to help us. Often the choice is made because they were like ourselves when on earth, and so have a sympathetic interest in our problems. Or it might be that they were concerned in a mission like our own, and feel they still have something useful to contribute. Whatever the reason, the motivation is love — but love that must always be detached from emotions. So in a sense, while *we* are being tried and tested, so are they, and one of their hardest tasks is to stand aside while watching us suffer some agonising lesson essential to our development.

It is probably this essential detachment that accounts for their desire to remain virtually anonymous. My Chinese teacher wished simply to be known as 'Chan', for his true name was unimportant. Whenever you hear of a Chinese helper he is invariably called Chan, and I thought this highly suspect until this perfectly logical explanation. They wish to completely lose their identity in the task of assisting us, and I suspect they consider our own names equally immaterial.

'He's of the Ming dynasty,' said Mr Mackay. 'I know this from the way he is dressed,' and he gave me a very detailed description which I noted down. This was in the early days of my seeking and, to be honest, I still had doubts, but months later I sat with Coral Polge, the psychic artist who had previously drawn a remarkable likeness of my youngest sister, while suffering (as sensitives often do) the symptoms of her last illness.

'You have a Chinese guide with you,' said Miss Polge. 'A very ancient gentleman,' and she proceeded to draw, with pastels, Chan as described by Mr Mackay. One particularly telling detail was the colour of a button on the top of his small round hat. 'He insists it is red.' Mackay had also said he attached importance to that button, saying it signified something of his position in life while on earth.

This was the third time Chan had been seen with me. Three different people had borne witness to him, so it was time to take his presence seriously. The pastel portrait, executed in a matter of minutes, showed a well-lined face with pronounced cheekbones, brown eyes, well-shaped mouth and long, straight wisp of a beard. The eyes were shrewd and kind, and the lips looked as if a smile lurked at the corners. A wise, compassionate, yet humorous countenance. I had the picture framed, hung it in my own sanctuary and then, when the warm glow crept over me, believed he was there.

Around that time a study group was formed among the Castle community. Under the direction of the Reverend John Crane, the plan was to investigate different religions, and clergymen of various denominations were invited to give talks. When they had exhausted all available sources of supply, I was asked to speak on Spiritualism and invited the group to my flat.

Our sanctuary was a large room furnished simply with chairs, and I added to these since the Healing Circle had offered their support. We were vaguely apprehensive while preparing for the visitors, for we knew a few were disapproving. It would be my first talk and I decided to tell, quite simply, of the events which had brought me to the Chapel.

The room looked peaceful and pleasant. Over the fireplace was a lovely picture of Christ which we felt might reassure the more orthodox members of the study group - and on the opposite wall the portrait of Chan, which might need some explaining! I doubted the wisdom of talking about guides at this early stage, and hoped the picture would not arouse their curiosity. An easy way to avoid this eventuality would have been to remove it, but no - if Chan was to help me in my time of need it was hardly the thing to banish his likeness to another room.

After the visitors had been made welcome, a few words were said to introduce me. I felt surprisingly calm and talked for perhaps forty minutes. It was not until afterwards, when asked to answer questions, that the disapproving members attacked my beliefs and sought to discredit them. I looked over their heads to Chan's picture and thought, 'If you are here to help me, now is the time'.

The warm glow crept over me, and to my surprise the answers to the awkward questions flashed into my mind, so I could reply without hesitation. Chan was helping, and has helped many times since. When I gave talks in the early days I would spend hours preparing notes, but soon realised they were not only restricting, but unnecessary. All that was needed was the faith to face an audience without preparation. Now I ask only to be given a subject, and rely on the inspiration of the moment, and answering questions is the part I enjoy most.

11

Healing is surely the most wonderful Spiritual gift and to some extent, within the reach of everyone. The main requisite is a love for humanity, and a man or woman who will listen, long and patiently, while distressed people unburden their troubles, is employing healing. The gift develops in strength according to one's desire to use it. Those who put aside a certain time for the task find the power increases, and this is because Spirit doctors, reassured as to the seriousness of their intent, keep the appointment with them, placing their knowledge and skill at their disposal.

My first misguided attempt at healing was a disaster, for I had rubbed the back of my predecessor and made him worse. True, I had followed his doctor's instructions, and it was a pity that my father, who was present at the time, could not actually stop me. But he was not a doctor, and must have wasted no time in consulting one, since Mrs Iles received the warning shortly after. Ideally, properly used healers will know instinctively if they are doing right.

Generally speaking, I was content to devote myself to distant healing, and leave the laying on of hands to others, but my friends on the other side seemed determined to give me *every* kind of experience and a new one was presented in the Chapel one Summer afternoon in 1970.

It was time for one of my breaks and I was passing under the organ screen, about to leave. A steady stream of visitors were pouring in and I noticed among them a woman and a boy. It was not a front view for they were walking away from me, but for some odd reason I seemed vividly aware of every detail of their appearance. The woman was hatless, dark-haired and of medium height, and she wore a navy blue anorak with a sheen upon it and narrow white edging, a blue skirt and sensible flat shoes.

The small boy hanging on her hand had what was once called a 'pudding basin' haircut and his brown hair had fairer streaks in it, as if bleached by the sun. His main feature, and misfortune, were his legs and feet, for the left leg was enclosed in a caliper while his right foot wore a thickly built-up shoe. He needed the woman's hand to steady him as he swung along, but he turned and looked up at her with an impish grin. A nice round, healthy face, full of mischief.

I felt a wave of compassion for this brave little lad and almost immediately an extraordinary thing happened, for I felt a distinct blow in the solar plexus, as if someone had struck me quite hard with a fist enclosed in a boxing glove. What could it mean? The solar plexus I knew was an important psychic centre, but why should the blow coincide with my feeling of pity for the boy? To draw attention to him, surely. But what was I to do about it?

It was one of the short breaks and I had much to do in the hour at my disposal, so I left the Chapel wishing I didn't have to. Perhaps I was meant to learn the boy's name and add it to our healing list. Several times, during the rest of the day, I reproached myself for not doing more.

And then, when out shopping next morning, who should I see approaching but the woman and the boy. They were dressed exactly as I'd seen them the day before, and this was the first time I'd had a front view of them. Clearly they were mother and son. It was the opportunity I'd hoped for, somehow I'd get the boy's name. But how? I could hardly go up to a stranger and ask for it. While I hesitated, I saw them enter Lyons Teashop. If only they would remain there a little while, I wasn't far from home, if I hurried I could write a short note, return and give it to the mother before they left. The letter was as difficult as it was urgent. 'Dear Madam - I saw you and your boy in the Chapel yesterday and was wondering if it might be possible to help him? We have a healing group which meets every week to pray for people, and we get surprising results, so might I have his name?'

I pushed the note into an envelope and hurried back to the teashop. It was only just in time, for they were getting up from their table. To my surprise I noticed there was another woman and a little girl with them. I said 'Hallo Sonny, I've seen you before!' and the boy grinned up at me. 'And this is for you,' I told his astonished mother, thrusting the letter into her hand. Unconventional it may have been, but I'd broken the ice, and we all left the shop together.

'I saw you in St George's Chapel yesterday,' I said by way of conversation.

The boy's mother paused, and looked at me incredulously. 'No, you must be mistaken. We've come up from Cardiff, just for the day.'

'I could swear I saw you both.'

'No, we were at home, making the arrangements. We did hope to see the Chapel and were up there just now, but there's a charge for admission and we can't afford it, so we're going for a walk along the river instead.'

I told them that if they used my name I'd arrange for them to be admitted, and then hurried back to work. Later in the day, standing under the organ screen, I saw them take advantage of my invitation. And now, as they walked away from me, they were *exactly* as I'd seen them the day before.

One of those odd tricks of time again. But why? Clearly it was to help the boy, so I asked them to tea at the flat and discovered his name was Francis Bowling. He sat beside me on the settee with his mother next to him, and his sister and aunt opposite. The laying on of hands, which I felt might be necessary, had to be stage-managed and was therefore a cursory affair. None of them knew anything of healing and I didn't even know if Mrs Bowling had read my note. And time was against me, for I was due back at the Chapel.

As if in fun, I knelt before the child and placed my hands on his legs, but I silently prayed that if there was healing in me it would flow into this brave little boy. I asked the mother is she would send me a photo of him and she did so, a black and white snapshot taken on the seashore, Francis dragging a piece of driftwood, happy and laughing, in spite of the caliper and heavy shoe. There was a short letter: 'I've taken Francis to the specialist and he says there's a big improvement. I can't really believe this has anything to do with our meeting, but I'm grateful all the same.'

Why should she believe? Anyway, it didn't matter, there had been a *big improvement.* This was followed by other good reports and finally, less than a year after meeting him, a colour snapshot of Francis on the beach at Tenby, without caliper or built-up shoe. 'Francis is fine. He continues in good health and his leg has improved no end,' wrote his mother. 'He's built up muscles and now there is only a slight shortness in his right leg. I'm sure a stranger would find it hard to believe he ever had a disability.'

It had been my great good fortune to be used as a channel, perhaps to prove I could do contact healing if I tried. But I had this strange feeling that the Spirit side of life were revealing many wonders to me *once,* to make me aware of them. Why? Why me? To write this account might be the explanation, but even as I put each experience on paper I find them, on reflection, almost unbelievable. And if I feel like this, how will the reader respond? Reject them, perhaps - unless they themselves have had a psychic experience which set them wondering. For strange things are happening to many people these days.

And why not? The word 'psychic' means 'of the soul', and since we all have souls, we are all psychic. But some are more aware of this than others, and the gifts of the spirit are found in the most unlikely individuals.

Take, for example, the 'discerning of spirits'. The rough youth who had sought solace at the Sanctuary had both seen, and heard, the malevolent woman at the inn. The young people in the haunted flat had seen the vindictive man. And to go further back, my practical, down-to-earth sister witnessed the ghost of 'Ada', while I, longing to make her acquaintance, had been unable to do so. Yet I have since seen many spirits when they transfigured mediums.

The gift of healing is far more evident in some people, and those who are not particularly keen on doing so have found they can benefit others by the laying on of hands.

Yet many, who long to heal, seem unable to do so. My encounter with the boy seemed a 'one off', for I have tried contact healing since with no tangible results.

At the time I felt instinctively that I was being shown: *'these things are possible', not* that it was in my power to make them happen. And there were further surprises in store.

☆ ☆ ☆

There are few things I dislike more than having my photograph taken, especially by a professional photographer. But sometimes it's necessary. I needed a new passport, and friends abroad, who hadn't seen me in years, were requesting my likeness, so I set out one day to make an appointment.

One of my policeman friends was on duty at the Henry VIII gateway. His name was Evan, one of the older men who did not enjoy good health and was not far from retirement. It was certainly not by chance that he should be there that morning, and free to have a word with me.

'You don't look happy,' he remarked, and I explained why.

'Perhaps I could help you out,' he offered. 'Photography's my hobby. I'll take them, if you like.' And it was arranged there and then that he would come to the flat later in the week.

The pictures were taken in the large end room we used as a Sanctuary, and Evan duly arrived with his son Glyn, a painfully shy teenager eager to act as his father's assistant. They brought with them a mass of equipment and converted the room into a studio in a matter of minutes.

The photographic session took nearly two hours, and it certainly wouldn't be their fault if there wasn't a worthwhile picture among them. Evan said he did his own developing and printing and would bring the results a few days later. True to his word, he brought dozens of prints and some were surprisingly good.

'Did you get any spirit extras?' I asked jokingly, but the jest fell flat since he didn't know what they were. I explained that 'ghosts' were said to sometimes appear on photographs.

'Nothing like that,' he said, sounding a little shocked at the idea. 'I did get odd lights on some.'

'How odd?'

'Just bright patches of light. I can't account for them. There's nothing wrong with my camera, and the lamps weren't angled in the direction they appear in.'

It sounded intriguing. 'I'd like to see them.'

'I think I've destroyed them all. They weren't any good. If I find one, I'll drop it in.'

A few days later, while on duty in the grounds, he slipped down to the flat and handed me an envelope. 'Can't stop - but here's what I promised you.'

It was a photo of me with a large oval patch of light beside my head. At one quick glance, it was just that, but as I looked longer, I saw there was a man's face enclosed in it. He had the appearance of a Biblical character with a full beard, a long rather hooked nose and dark, piercing eyes. The longer I looked, the plainer it seemed to become.

I hurried to find Evan and found him patrolling the terraces. 'Take a good look at that patch of light and tell me what you see.'

As he studied the photograph I was fascinated to see a flood of perspiration pour down from under his helmet. 'It's a man's face!' he gasped.

'Describe him to me.'

'He's got long hair and a full beard,' he started, then: 'I tell you what he looks like to me — one of the old prophets. Like Moses.'

Exactly. The face was there. Assuredly, it had to be looked for. At first glance it was purely a patch of light, and when Evan made further prints, some were less good and the face more difficult to find.

He phoned me next evening. 'If you're not doing anything, could you come round? I'd like you to meet the rest of the family, and there's something we want you to see.' I detected a note of excitement.

Evan lived in one of the police houses on the edge of the Great Park and here I met his attractive wife, their married son, Brian, and his pretty wife, Mary. The shy Glyn hovered in the background. What they had to show me was a dining-room table scattered with prints of my photograph and they were all highly excited. Apart from the old man, they were finding more 'extras', not in patches of light, but often in the shadows. They had traced them over with a pencil.

Even allowing for an occasional excess of imagination, they managed to find at least a dozen acceptable faces and figures. There was even an animal shape on the floor which I naturally hoped might be Simon. Finally, having exhausted all possibilities, we settled down to talk and I told them how I had been brought into this understanding.

'I'm so happy about it all,' said Mary. 'I've always had a fear of death and now I haven't.'

Something had happened to that little family that evening, and they were all happily aware of it. One of them asked if I'd say a prayer before leaving. It was a turning point in the lives of five people, and they were never to look back.

After consulting the rest of the group I suggested Evan and his family should join the Circle and they gladly did so. Apart from Brian and Mary, the others were in real need of healing and the improvement in their health was remarkable. The Police Inspector, who was now a good friend, knew the family better than I and commented on the change: 'Joining your Circle has certainly done wonders,' he said. 'One or the other was always ill. If it wasn't Evan himself it was his wife or the boy. You wouldn't know they were the same people now, they're not only fit and well, they're so much more confident.'

When Evan retired, they all moved to Jersey which was Mary's home, and there they started a Healing Circle in which they were all happily involved. So you see now why that man was on duty when I went to have my photograph taken. It was to help him and his family and then bring then to the point where they could help others.

And through those photographs came something more, for a friend who heard about them phoned to say her son had recently taken some snapshots which also appeared to have something unaccountable on them.

Stephen Woollard, a keen young photographer with an excellent camera, was visiting Beaulieu in Hampshire one Summer afternoon when he saw an attractive archway in the Abbey ruins and decided to photograph it. When the colour prints were developed he found three had horizontal orange streaks across them. Two looked so bad he destroyed them, but luckily he kept the third and sent it to me.

It shows a procession of nine monks, their cowled heads clearly visible while their bodies dissolved into light. I had heard of the monks of Beaulieu and decided to spend a brief holiday there to investigate. Lord Montagu was naturally interested in the picture, and was aware that many local residents claimed to have seen the ghosts, often in broad daylight, strolling about or sitting on benches. *He* had not seen them. With his permission I was allowed to roam the ruins at night with my tape recorder, but unfortunately had no more than the enjoyable experience of walking under the stars in that lovely, peaceful place.

But one thing bothered me. Why were the monks still haunting Beaulieu? Surely as enlightened religious men they should have journeyed on? And then I remembered there were such things as 'psychic shells'. They exist in such places as the Tower of London. Anne Boleyn, seen without her head, is *not* an earthbound spirit, the poor soul has moved on long ago. What people have seen is her 'psychic shell.' I can only describe this as a horrific impression left by her terror on the atmosphere. Meeting it must be like walking into a room and being confronted with a ghastly portrait.

Praying for an answer concerning the monks I awoke with what I believe to be the explanation. What people see are their gentle, unfrightening shells, left behind, not through horror, but happiness. Isn't it possible they found great joy in their brotherhood, serving God and man in that beautiful place?

The photograph inspired me, at long last, to return to writing with a radio play called '*Figures in the Foreground*'. The fact that the BBC accepted it as offered showed a healthy change in their attitude during the past few years. Once they would have suggested the psychic phenomena in the story should be accounted for by some human agency, but now it was allowed to remain as written.

Shaun Usher, a witty investigative journalist, wrote an

article about the play in the *Daily Mail*. He asked 'Is there a ghost in your family album?' and to judge by the numbers of letters received many people sought the answer with varying results.

Little by little, the truth filters through. Books, plays and films dealing with fraudulent mediums and fake phenomena are things of the past. Spiritual enlightenment increases and gains the respectful consideration long deserved.

It was around this time the *Sunday Express* published six intelligent, thought-provoking articles dealing with Reincarnation. Half a dozen people wrote of recurring dreams in childhood (usually nightmares) which suggested the manner in which their last life came to an end.

Although the other members of the Circle had not read the articles, I thought it an interesting topic for discussion and asked if any of them had had recurring dreams when they were young. Two of them had.

'I used to dream I was marched out of a building, stood up against a wall and shot,' said David, who sang in the Chapel choir. 'It scared me, naturally. I still get the dream sometimes, but it doesn't worry me now. I just say to myself, 'Here's that dream again!'

'I think I can beat that,' said Maureen. 'I used to dream I was a soldier on a battle-field, but I wasn't wearing a British uniform, at least not as we know them these days. I had a rifle with a fixed bayonet and was thoroughly enjoying myself, killing the enemy.'

She didn't remember being killed herself, I suspect that in the heat of the moment, she didn't even notice. Maureen is a pretty, very feminine young woman and the idea of her as a soldier on a battle-field amused us.

'Do you still get the dream?' someone asked.

'Sometimes. I always enjoy it when I do, and there's nothing I enjoy more than a war film.'

In a significant number of apparent reincarnation cases the previous life ended violently or prematurely. Believers maintain that this does not mean that only those who meet violent deaths are reincarnated, but simply that those who die a natural death, particularly in old age, do not carry over distinct memories from one life to another. Violent death, it seems, can leave strong impressions not only on the soul, but also in some cases on the physical body. Several researchers have noted birthmarks in the alleged reincarnates situated where fatal wounds were sustained in the previous life.

If I had known of this at the time, I would have asked David and Maureen if they had any interesting birthmarks, but the information came later in the work of Professor Ian Stevenson. An American physician and psychiatrist, he has contributed to several branches of parapsychology and written a book called '*Twenty Cases Suggestive of Reincarnation*' based on his own intensive research into the subject.

I recalled no recurring dreams but remembered that unaccountable behaviour as a boy — making a cross and hiding it in a secret place. One evening at the Sanctuary of St John, the monk who had kept me informed about Len came to say goodbye. Len was now safely delivered into other hands and his care of him had ended. I thanked him for his messages.

'He says you don't have to thank him. He's been happy to repay an old debt. He wants you to know his name is Brother Bernard. You were together in a monastery in Brussels, and you nursed him when he was sick.'

This was before the sitting with William Redmond in which he told me of that earlier life. I had asked why we didn't remember more of a previous existence. He explained it would be too much of a burden, the life we were living *now* was what mattered, but we retained within us the total sum of what we had learned earlier. That seemed to make sense.

Those who do not believe in reincarnation may point out that the word doesn't appear in the Bible. I think it possible the word hadn't been coined at the time, but if you study the good book carefully you will find things which cannot be explained unless you accept rebirth as a fact.

To quote just one: In St Matthew, Chapter 16, verses 13 and 14, we read: 'when Jesus came into the coast of Caesarea Phillipi, he asked his disciples, saying "who do people say that I, the son of man, am?" and they said, "Some say that thou art John the Baptist, some Elias, and others Jeremias, or one of the other prophets."'

All the men referred to had died years before, so how can we interpret this in any other way? Jesus had phrased the question expecting that people would be speculating that another soul was reborn in Him, and they had replied accordingly. So I think we can safely conclude that rebirth was an accepted fact in those far-off times.

And why not? The forerunners of Christ had believed in it and it is a fundamental part of the Hindu and Buddhist religions. What I find curious is the fact that millions of people in the East continue to believe in it to this day, while the Western world seemed inclined to drop the idea and are only now showing a renewed interest in it again.

12

My life as a Sacristan at St George's Chapel lasted, surprisingly, for seven years. I had found it, from the first, quite strenuous, and if it hadn't been for the Circle, and the support of friends, I wouldn't have stayed the course as long as I did. The Dean and Canons assured me they accepted my resignation with regret, and gave a farewell party in my honour.

I was joining the Seeker's Trust, a long established religious community in Kent, devoted to spiritual healing. While looking forward to a less arduous life, it was sad to leave so many friends, and my home within the Castle walls.

The good and faithful Ken Taylor undertook to continue the Circle elsewhere, and a kind lady offered the use of a room nearby, but things were never the same, and it eventually closed. I think the spiritual power within Marbeck House had been stronger than we realised. The fact remains, it had been a source of strength, comfort and healing to innumerable people. Some of the sick who attended became healers themselves, while others began their own Circles, here and abroad, working on similar lines.

A lovely bond of friendship continues to exist between all who were ever linked with it.

☆ ☆ ☆

When making the decision to leave Windsor, I knew it was not only the start of a new life, but the end of an adventure. My loved ones, who I'd long considered 'dead and gone', had known of my desperate needs, and come forward to help me. Why? Out of love. *Love is the key to everything.* Now they considered I could take care of myself, and returned to their own lives. But during the time they were with me they had made their presence felt, and I missed the warm glow — the feeling they were still somewhere around.

I knew I had only to seek a sitting with a reliable medium to make contact with 'the other side', but I was determined not to be forever seeking this reassurance. Every instinct tells me we should not do this. We are here to learn, and must do so with the aid of our own God-given spirit.

The help given me was unsought for, but extremely necessary, not only for my physical needs, but as a means of bringing me into this truth; but we are here for our spiritual growth and must not expect to be guided each step of the way by spirits wiser than ourselves. Neither should we be too preoccupied with thoughts of the *next* world. While we may not always like this one, we belong to it while we are here, and it is part of our mission to contribute, in some way, to making it a better place, working through our relationships with others.

Somewhere within us is the total sum of all we have learned in previous incarnations, and we hopefully have grown a little in the likeness of Christ, but still lessons remain to be learned, or we would not have returned to the school of life. We are facing another end-of-term examination, but if some loving but misguided spirit gave us the answers they would render a disservice which might involve a further visit to the earth plane. I prefer the prospects in the realms of spirit, which might be likened to a college of further education in happier circumstances.

It was the so-called death of my friend and teacher that had opened up these wonders for me, and I would end with some final messages concerning him.

Brother Bernard, who had helped him through his redemption, had said his work was finished and 'he was safely delivered into other hands'. I wondered hopefully, what this could mean. Len had been an unwanted child, and this was largely responsible for his tragedy. I had prayed in the early days that my parents would adopt him, and it was in a little room in Belgrave Square that I finally heard the answer to that prayer.

The medium was the remarkable Nora Blackwood. Unhappily no longer with us, she was a much sought-after sensitive in her time, and it was necessary to book an appointment months in advance. Even so, it was not a private sitting. I was one of a group of six, but the few minutes devoted to me personally were certainly memorable.

'I have your Mother and your Father here, and there's a young man standing between them. I get the name "Len". But wasn't there something else you called him?' She was listening intently. 'No — I can't get it! Jumble? Bumble?', she almost laughed. 'It can't be "Mumble"?'

'It was.' I told her, and joined in the laughter, overjoyed at this evidence and the thought of the three of them together.

Mrs Blackwood was quickly serious again. 'He became a little emotional when you spoke, and your father is comforting him - he puts an arm about his shoulders and is saying, "Now, now Len, you mustn't upset yourself." And now your mother is asking me to tell you: "This is what you prayed for, isn't it? He was a lost soul when *you* found him, and a lost soul when *we* found him, but he isn't lost any more."'

I was overwhelmed by this wonderful answer to prayer.

Len never failed to make an appearance in every sitting afterwards, and in each one he became happier and more progressed. In the early days all the communications were overshadowed by the tragedy of his suicide. He could not forgive himself. Sometimes he could not bear to speak of it, and at others he talked of nothing else. Filled with remorse, he was desperately afraid I might in some way blame myself for his death. 'He wants you to know you did all you could. It was not your fault, you couldn't have prevented it. It was bound to happen.'

Strangely, while I had tried to understand when he was with me, it was through sensitives that I got a true insight into his character. 'He could not love himself,' said Inga Hooper, in a sitting, several years later. 'But he's happy now and often with you. He says, if it hadn't happened, you wouldn't have gained this knowledge, and it's for you to bring it into the lives of others. He's speaking of writing. He knows you have kept careful notes and hopes you will use them for a book which will help people.'

'If I attempted such a thing, has he any idea what I should call it?'

There was a pause, then: 'He says you were always good at thinking of titles for your plays.'

'But this would be far more important than a play.'

'He nods in agreement.' She listened for a few minutes, then added: 'It was his death that was the means of showing you that life continues. Doesn't that suggest something?'

A matter of life and death, I thought, but in reverse order. I was too busy at that time to consider writing anything, but it may be said that the seed had been sown at that time.

During my years at St George's Chapel I met, and talked to, thousands of people. There were the large parties of tourists who filled the vast nave, waiting for a lecture, and this was always an ordeal since the sound system wasn't reliable. Finally I learned to manage without a microphone, and this experience in public speaking was to prove useful when I came to give talks on the experiences recounted here.

More enjoyable were the quieter occasions when it was possible to talk to a few people at a time. A separate book could be written on this alone. Variety was certainly the spice of life where our visitors were concerned, for they ranged from foreign royalty to politicians and film stars. If we read in the paper of a celebrity visiting this country for the first time, we knew there was every chance that they'd 'take-in' the Chapel and Castle before departing again.

The most important visitor as far as I was concerned was a charming, scholarly American, Dr Stanley C. Searle. A true anglophile, he came to this country as often as possible, and visited the Chapel two days in succession to learn more of its history. Luckily it was autumn, which meant we were less busy, so it was possible to give him individual attention.

How we got on the subject of Spiritualism is something I forget, but I lent him a book on the subject which he read with interest. Not surprisingly, he found it hard to believe, but our Circle was soon to be visited by Muriel Miller, and I remember saying: 'Please don't tell me anything about yourself. Come along and meet this lady. I think she may surprise you.'

Eight of us sat with Muriel on the evening of his visit and she, as always, divided the time equally between us. She started with Dr Searle, her face transfiguring to that of an elderly man while her voice became male and gently American. To our delight, this newcomer was answering as if it were the most natural thing in the world. He was talking to his father, and it was a fascinating conversation.

'You know, my son, I'm concerned about your mother. Her illness has not been properly diagnosed. You should change her doctor, or at least get a second opinion.'

'I've been thinking about doing that, Dad,' said the man who had come with such doubts about Spiritualism.

Since the following ten minutes dealt with private matters, it is sufficient to say that the spirit of his father spoke of many things that only Dr Searle knew about, and we were all aware of the concern and affection between them. I was glad I had asked my new friend to tell me nothing, for it made what transpired startlingly evidential. For my part, I had learned not only of his parents but the fact that he taught at a school situated in New Jersey.

Later, he wrote from America: 'I have been telling my students, in the philosophy class, of my extraordinary experiences in England, and they are naturally interested. They would like to know more about Spiritualism. Can you recommend any books which might be helpful, or somewhere in New York where they might learn more? What I would really like is for you to talk to them, for it is a genuine interest, and I'd like to satisfy their curiosity.'

A few weeks later the game I played as a child became a reality. My 'bricks' had become twenty bright teenagers and I found myself, a very happy teacher, in a class room at the Ranney School, New Jersey.

☆ ☆ ☆

'We can't really believe all you tell us,' said one of the girls in the philosophy class.

'I didn't come all the way from England to tell you fairy tales,' I replied.

The girl coloured, and the rest of the class all began talking at once. We had only known each other a few days but already a comradeship existed between us.

'Terry didn't mean that we don't believe *you*,' said one of the boys. 'We all believe these things happened to you personally, but we can't really accept them unless they happen to us.'

They were all in agreement and most concerned that I shouldn't be offended. It was perfectly understandable.

The incident came at the end of the first week, and there must have been unseen witnesses who saw my difficulty and quickly arranged a few things to turn the tide in my favour. During the remaining weeks of my visit, some of the young people were to have strange experiences as puzzling as mine.

Perhaps the most intriguing happened to Connie Pappayliou. Connie had gone to the Great Adventure, a pleasure ground in New Jersey, accompanied by a school friend Joanne Ricci. When they left, Connie took a wrong turning on leaving the car park and after driving a number of miles realized they were well and truly lost. The girls tried to laugh and joke about their predicament but were really becoming quite alarmed, for the hour was late. Finally, in desperation, they decided to find a phone box in the next township, call the police, and so discover the way home.

On being connected with the police station a voice asked: 'Are you the two girls from Tom's River who've lost yourselves?' Tom's River was Joanne's home, but when Connie was about to explain that they were certainly lost, the voice told them to stay where they were, and a police car arrived shortly after to put them on the right road.

The astonished girls asked the policeman how he knew they were lost, and he said they had received a call at the station giving the information, and saying exactly where to find them.

Connie came to the class so eager to tell of the adventure that there was no point in starting until she'd finished. 'No one knew we were lost but ourselves!' she said incredulously. 'When I got home I woke my mother and asked if she'd been worried, but she said she'd gone to bed and didn't even know how late it was. Joanne's parents weren't anxious either.'

And even if the parents had alerted the police, it wouldn't account for the call being traced to that little town, and the location of the phone box.

'You told us there were guardian angels and spirits who watch over us,' said the excited Connie. 'And I certainly believe it now.'

All the young people in that class were about to continue their education elsewhere, and one girl was concerned because she'd been told the accommodation at the University of her choice would be one small, dreary room. This worried her considerably. Then she had a dream in which she visited the place and was shown not one room but two, one leading from the other. The larger had a window seat and lovely views. When she visited the University a few days later the accommodation was just as she'd seen it in her dream, and she was delighted.

Something else was to happen to strengthen my case. One afternoon an elderly, serious-looking gentleman looked round the door, introduced himself as a member of the staff and asked if he might sit in on the lesson. I had no choice but to agree but felt a little daunted by his presence. It would have worried me even more had I known he was, in fact, the Director of Religious Studies.

It was the session in which I touched on the subject of 'Spirit extras' in photographs and had brought the controversial picture of the monks of Beaulieu as an example. Our visitor, who had made no comments all afternoon, suddenly broke his silence. 'Oh, there's no doubt that the photograph *is genuine*,' he asserted airily. 'I was once a Cistercian monk and I've walked in a procession like that many times. They are on the way to the burial ground. Would you know where that is?' (I didn't know then, but have checked since, and yes, they *are* walking in that direction.)

The Ranney School produced a beautiful Year Book with photographs of all the students and staff. I was given one, autographed by all the people I met, and the comments of the boys and girls in the philosophy class are warm-hearted, thoughtful and sincere.

Will the experiences related here be of use to those young people, or, for that matter, anyone else who may read them? I hope so. Not only when confronted with the loss of a loved one (which we must all face sooner or later) but at other times of trouble. Life grows increasingly difficult, and if we believe a struggle for existence in the materialistic world is all there is, we may well despair and feel tempted to give up the struggle.

But it is NOT all there is.

POSTSCRIPT

A book entitled *Windsor in the War - a Domestic Chronicle. 1939-1945.* by Angus Macnaghten, is an edited collection of letters written by his mother while he was on active service. I suspect that Hazel Macnaghten, like all kind and considerate mothers, carefully avoided the unhappier side of life on the Home Front, and her account of goings on in the Royal Borough is both lively and entertaining.

I was especially interested in her references to my old and valued friend, Constance Crispe, since I knew nothing of her activities during the war, and didn't even know if the Sanctuary had existed at that time. But here it is:

'Mrs Crispe is an ardent Spiritualist, and many meetings and seances provided comfort and excitement. I went to a sort of Spiritualist meeting in her drawing room today. The usual stuff and very drawn out. There were two mediums there, and I ended up with a perfectly black baby being put into my lap by a Spirit. I am afraid I greeted this with laughter, but the medium informed me it was a most radiant infant, and a very lucky symbol. They talk such a lot of rot.

'At tea, one medium went under control, and spoke with a foreign accent, supposed to be an Egyptian, living two thousand years ago. I believe in the Spirit World, but all this is very unconvincing as far as *I* am concerned.' Then, later: 'My Mother allowed Mrs Crispe and some friends to hold a seance at the house, but the proceedings were not very interesting or convincing. A spirit of an old man was very annoyed with Minna for not remembering him, when she was two years old.' And finally: 'A bomb fell near

Langley, woke them all out of their trances, and the spirits fled.'

Then, at last, a more impressive entry.

'Mrs Crispe and some friends came to hold another seance in Hadleigh House. The medium was controlled for a long while by Goldilocks, a nasty little infant spirit, who laughs shrilly, and talks in a high, childish voice - most precocious. More interesting was the case of a Military Knight, who "came through". He had died quite recently. The description of him was so good, and the voice and manner so like him, that I immediately recognised Colonel Egan. He said he didn't know why no-one would speak to him now, as he was always seeing people in the streets who he knew, so he was glad he could talk to us. He can't realize he's dead.'

So here, at last, is proof of survival. Colonel Egan had lived in one of the grace-and-favour houses that face St George's Chapel at Windsor Castle. At least one of these was reputed to be haunted -perhaps by the Colonel while in this unhappy state. But to return to the book:

'A seance at Mrs Crispe's was marred by the medium's control speaking in rhyme for two hours — most trying for me, as I loathe poetry, except in very small doses. But the medium, a Mrs Murphy, was quite impressive. I hear Norman Birkett put a lot of intricate legal points to her, when she was in trance, and she answered in a most astonishing and convincing way, which quite dumbfounded him.'

Who was the 'impressive' Mrs Murphy? Doubtless she was one of those humble, hard-working mediums who brought help and comfort to many, for little or no financial gain, for in those days it was not quite the thing to make money out of mediumship. There even existed a fear that the spiritual gift would be removed if exploited in that manner.

The gentleman who was dumbfounded is well documented. The Right Honourable Sir (William) Norman Birkett, QC, was considered one of the ablest and more prominent members of the English Bar. So these last quotes from Mrs Macnaghten's letters more than compensate for the shortcomings expressed earlier.

☆ ☆ ☆

Constance Crispe died, after a long and painful illness, on 29 June 1970. She had cancer and was nursed in her own home by the faithful Elsie Cripps, who, at her insistence, continued to hold the services in the Sanctuary, which was next to her bedroom. We sang hymns unaccompanied, which was not a success.

One Sunday evening I persuaded one of our Circle to play the piano for us. The young man, Jason Smart, was assistant organist at the Chapel, and more than willing to oblige. He played and we sang with relish, hoping the lady would appreciate our efforts from her sick-bed, but unhappily, although we were unaware of the fact, Jason was taking the hymns at a spanking pace which didn't meet with her approval.

Towards the end, the poor lady refused drugs, and when I saw her she was propped up in bed, bright-eyed and still, to my mind, beautiful. She was clearly in pain and when I sympathized she smiled and said, gently: 'What is my suffering, compared with that of Our Lord?'

A Christian Spiritualist, in the true sense, I can never think of her without recalling the words she placed above her door: *'All Seekers after the Truth are welcome here.'* The courage that prompted her to open her home to all and sundry remained with her until the end.